❧ WHO WROTE THE GOSPELS? ❧

This book is dedicated to my friend Bruce Mazet whose help and encouragement made it possible.

WHO WROTE THE ❧ GOSPELS? ❧

by Randel McCraw Helms

MILLENNIUM PRESS

MILLENNIUM PRESS
ALTADENA, CALIFORNIA

Quotations from the Bible in English,
unless otherwise noted, come from the *New English Bible* (1976).

Quotations from the Greek Septuagint version of the Hebrew Bible
(herein abbreviated LXX) come from *The Septuagint with Apocrypha: Greek and English*,
ed. Lancelot C. L. Brenton (Grand Rapids: Zondervan, 1980; orig. London, 1851).

Quotations from the Greek New Testament come from Erwin Nestle, *Novum
Testamentum Grecae* (26th ed. by Kurt Aland et al.; Stuttgart:
Deutsche Bibelstiftung, 1979).

Copyright © 1997 Randel Helms

Published in the United States by Millennium Press,
2761 North Marengo Ave., Altadena, California, 91001.
Phone: 626/794-3119; Fax: 626/794-1301; e-mail: skepticmag@aol.com

Library of Congress Cataloging-in-Publication Data

Helms, Randel
Who Wrote the Gospels?
Includes Bibliographical Reference and Index
ISBN: 0-9655047-2-7

Library of Congress Catalog Card Number: 96-078370
1. Gospel/Bible history. 2. Biblical criticism. 3. Ancient history

Book design, illustrations, chart, map, and jacket design by Pat Linse
Edited by Betty McCollister and Michael Shermer

Cover Painting: *The Seven Gospel Writers*. Art by Pat Linse

9 8 7 6 5 4 3 2 1

Printed in the United States of America on acid-free paper

First Edition
second printing

CONTENTS

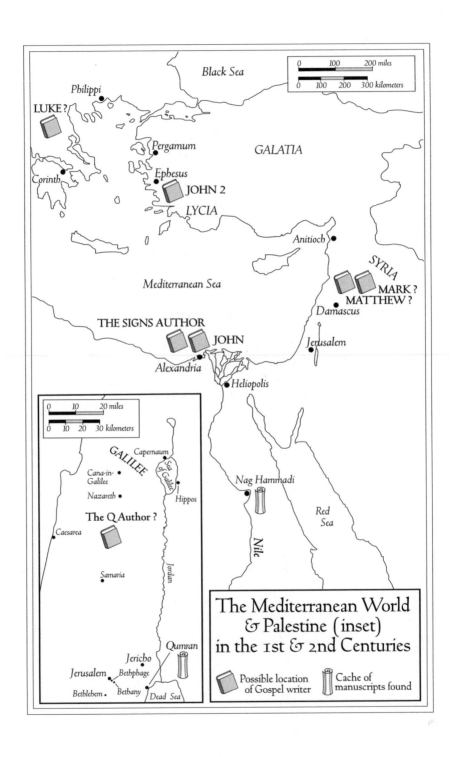

Black Sea

0   100   200 miles
0   100   200   300 kilometers

Philippi
LUKE ?

Pergamum

GALATIA

Corinth

Ephesus
JOHN 2

LYCIA

Anitioch

SYRIA
MARK ?
MATTHEW ?

Mediterranean Sea

Damascus

THE SIGNS AUTHOR

JOHN

Jerusalem

Alexandria

Heliopolis

0   10   20 miles
0   10   20   30 kilometers

GALILEE   Capernaum

Cana-in-
Galilee
Nazareth

Sea of Galilee

Hippos

Nag Hammadi

The Q Author ?

Caesarea

Red
Sea

Samaria

Jordan

Nile

Jericho   Qumran
Jerusalem   Bethphage
Bethlehem .   Bethany
Dead Sea

The Mediterranean World
& Palestine (inset)
in the 1st & 2nd Centuries

Possible location   Cache of
of Gospel writer   manuscripts found

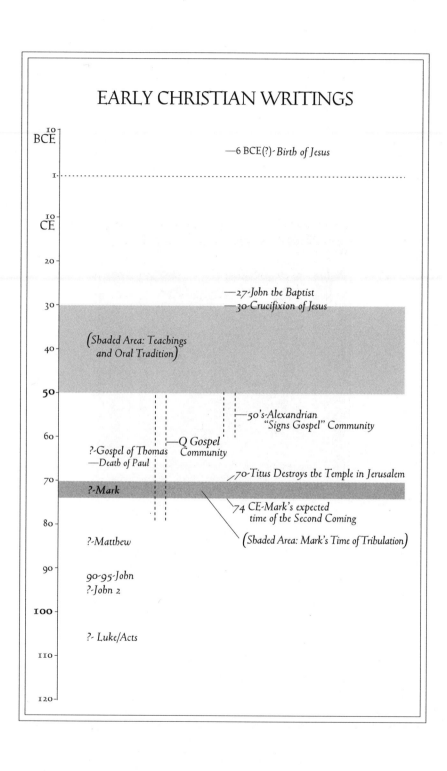

EARLY CHRISTIAN WRITINGS

10 BCE

—6 BCE(?)· Birth of Jesus

1

10 CE

20

—27·John the Baptist
—30·Crucifixion of Jesus

30

(Shaded Area: Teachings
and Oral Tradition)

40

50

—50's·Alexandrian
"Signs Gospel" Community

60

?·Gospel of Thomas
—Death of Paul

—Q Gospel
Community

—70·Titus Destroys the Temple in Jerusalem

70

?·Mark

74 CE·Mark's expected
time of the Second Coming

80

?·Matthew

(Shaded Area: Mark's Time of Tribulation)

90

90-95·John
?·John 2

100

?· Luke/Acts

110

120

Introduction

Who Wrote The Gospels?

NO ONE would trouble to ask such a question if it were not that all four of the biblical gospels are deliberately, even playfully, anonymous in their texts. The Third Gospel for example carefully names its audience, Theophilus ("Friend of God"—Luke 1:3), but never its author; while the last chapter of the Fourth Gospel takes great pains to identify the author of that work as "the disciple whom Jesus loved" (John 21:7, 20), and then never tells us his name! The gospels are so anonymous that their titles, all second-century guesses, are all four wrong. Christians in the second century, possessing anonymous manuscripts and eager to give names to them, fastened upon four historical figures—the Apostles Matthew and John, Luke the "beloved physician" of Paul (Col. 4:14), and John Mark of Jerusalem, the "son" of Peter (Acts 12:12; I Peter 5:13). It's relatively easy to show that these identifications are imaginary and based on wishful thinking, and I will do so below. But that really is not the most amazing part: what still surprises is that, paradoxically, though the four gospels are anonymous they in fact tell us more about their authors than they do about their ostensible subject, the historical Jesus of Nazareth.

If the paragraph above surprises you, welcome to the ongoing debate; biblical scholarship is still chewing on the truly groundbreaking argument of Rudolf Bultmann, propounded some seventy years ago, that any gospel is

> a primary source for the historical situation out of which it arose, and is only a secondary source for the historical details concerning which it gives information. (Bultmann, 1960, 38)

That the gospels tell us more about the situations of their origin than about their subject is a disturbing idea, and remains controversial. As

Introduction

Robert Funk has recently put it:

> Biblical scholars have not been able to make up their minds whether the biblical narra-
> tives are about real or fictive events. Or, if they are about both, which is which. The test
> is a simple one: did the events depicted as having taken place actually take place? Are the
> gospels essentially fiction or biography? (Funk, 1997, 179)

The title of my last book on this subject, *Gospel Fictions* (Helms, 1988),
gives some idea of my own views, but there is much more to be said about
the authors of the gospels. There is a gradually growing consensus that
since, as John Meier puts it in his recent biography of Jesus, the gospels are
"1st century Greco-Roman religious propaganda" (Meier, 1991, 419) "the
real Jesus is unknown and unknowable. The real Jesus is not available and
never will be" (22); thus our efforts to recover what is recoverable about
the historical Jesus can give us only a "fragmentary hypothetical recon-
construction" (31). Likewise, in another major biography of Jesus published the same year as Meier's, John Dominic Crossan reminds us that in
"the search for the historical Jesus...there is *only* reconstruction" (Crossan,
1991, 426).

No one should be surprised at Meier's description of the gospels as
"religious propaganda"; for the Gospel of John (20:30-31) frankly declares
this as its purpose:

> There were indeed many other signs that Jesus performed in the presence of his disci-
> ples, which are not recorded in this book. Those here written have been recorded in
> order that you may hold the faith that Jesus is the Christ, the Son of God, and that
> through this faith you may possess life by his name.

The gospels were written to convert or confirm their readers to Christianity
(surely no shameful project); they are the highly colored arguments of
powerful authors, not just transparent windows upon the historical Jesus.
If we adjust our focus from the brilliant imaginative pictures to the imag-
inations that produced them, to the situations out of which they arose, we
get to the point of this book—a study of the minds of the authors we call
Matthew, Mark, Luke, and John.

Introduction

Let me state my thesis now. Behind these four names I count seven authors: six men and one woman. No one can supply their names, but I do hope to describe their minds, their thought-processes and world views, how they wrote and how they viewed their sources of information about Jesus.

A word about my presuppositions: I assume the validity of the Two-Source Theory (that the authors of Matthew and Luke wrote with copies of the Gospel of Mark and the Sayings Gospel Q open in front of them, copying large amounts of both works). Of Mark's 666 verses, some 600 appear in Matthew, some 300 in Luke. Any careful reading of the three Synoptic Gospels (that is, Matthew, Mark and Luke) in some such work as Robert Funk's *New Gospel Parallels* (1985) will reveal that Mark is the common element between Matthew and Luke and was a source for both of them. I also agree with such scholars as Arland Jacobson that the "non-Markan passages common to both Matthew and Luke agree word-for-word so often that Q must have been a written document and not simply a body of material that Matthew and Luke took from oral tradition" (Miller, 1992, 249). And that there are works of three different authors inside the Gospel of John will surprise some, but not those who have read such standard commentaries on this gospel as those by Bultmann (1971) and Haenchen (1984). I will look at the Four in the order of their completion—Mark, Matthew, Luke-Acts, John—with a brief excursion into two "lost gospels," Thomas and Q. If you finish this book, I think you will be able to answer the question of its title.

❦ I ❦

WHO WROTE THE GOSPEL OF MARK?

JUDGING BY THE NOTORIETY of the names of the gospel authors—Matthew, Mark, Luke, and John—one would think we must know a great deal about them. Not so. Let's consider what we know and do not know about the author of the Gospel of Mark. Starting with his name in the work's Greek title, *KATA MARKON*, we discover that the title is, in fact, a second-century guess. Eusebius, in his fourth-century *History of the Church*, gives us the story. In Book III of his work, Eusebius reports that in the fragments of the writings of Papias, the second-century Bishop of Hierapolis, this figure remarked that he was always interested in what any Christian visitor to his city might tell him about the old days of the first-century church:

> And whenever anyone came who had been a follower of the presbyters, I inquired into the words of the presbyters, what Andrew or Peter had said, or Philip or Thomas or James or John or Matthew, or any other disciple of the Lord, and what Ariston and the presbyter John, disciples of the Lord, were still saying. For I did not imagine that things out of books would help me as much as the utterances of a living and abiding voice. (150)

Papias was, in other words, a collector of oral lore about early Christianity, of which there was a great abundance. Eusebius notes that Papias "reproduces other stories communicated to him by word of mouth, together with some otherwise unknown parables and teachings of the Saviour"; indeed, Eusebius continues, Papias apparently got his "notions by misinterpreting the apostolic accounts," since he "seems to have been a man of very small intelligence, to judge from his books" (152-153). Having thus described Papias, Eusebius then adds "a piece of information which he sets out regarding Mark, the writer of the gospel":

Who Wrote The Gospels?

This, too, the presbyter used to say. "Mark, who had been Peter's interpreter, wrote down carefully, but not in order, all that he remembered of the Lord's sayings and doings. For he had not heard the Lord or been one of His followers, but later, as I said, one of Peter's." (152).

So already by the second century it was thought that though the author of the Gospel of Mark was not an eyewitness of Jesus he was the personal associate of someone who was. But note the third-hand nature of this information: a "presbyter" believed that Mark wrote down Peter's memories, a notion that Papias recorded and Eusebius copied from his writings. We can best compare this second-century guess with Luke's first-century statement about Peter and John Mark. According to Acts, when Peter escaped from prison in Jerusalem, "he made for the house of Mary, the mother of John Mark" (Acts 12:12). Later in the same chapter, Barnabas and Paul left Jerusalem for Antioch, "taking John Mark with them" (12:25). So the author of Luke-Acts not only knew about a John Mark of Jerusalem, the personal associate of Peter and Paul, but also possessed a copy of what we call the Gospel of Mark, copying some three hundred of its verses into the Gospel of Luke, and never once thought to link the two—John Mark and the Gospel of Mark—together! The reason is simple: the connecting of the

---

HOW MARK WROTE—THE STUFF OF LEGEND OR PERSONAL MEMORY?

• Not Peter, but Christian legend, was Mark's source about John the Baptist.

• Mark says, "In the prophet Isaiah it stands written," and then quotes a garbled blending of Exodus 23:20 and Malachi 3:1. Oral tradition does this kind of blending, not Peter's memory.

• Christians wanted John the Baptist to be the "herald" promised by Malachi, "the prophet Elijah" who would be sent "before the great and terrible day of the LORD" (Mal. 4:5), so they depicted John precisely as Elijah was seen in the Bible, "girt with a leather girdle about his loins" (II Kings 1:8; Mark 1:6). The stuff of legend here again, not personal memory.

I: Who Wrote the Gospel of Mark?

anonymous Gospel of Mark with John Mark of Jerusalem is a second-century guess, one that had not been made in Luke's time. The gospel we call Mark was in fact as anonymous to Luke as it is to us. Indeed, nowhere in their texts do any of the four gospels name their writers; their present titles are all second-century guesses about anonymous first-century works.

That the author of Mark was anything but a close associate of Peter is most clearly seen in the text of the gospel itself. Most of the Gospel of Mark is a collection of what had previously been unconnected fragments about Jesus, units of oral tradition, and brief written stories and sayings that reveal a long history of transmission before they reached Mark; the collection looks nothing like the "reminiscences" of Peter, though its lack of a clear chronology accounts for Papias' sense that it is "not in order." The opening verses of Mark show clearly their origin in a pre-Markan account rather than in Peter's memory:

> In the prophet Isaiah it stands written: "Here is my herald whom I send on ahead of you, and he will prepare your way. A voice crying aloud in the wilderness, 'Prepare a way for the Lord; clear a straight path for him.'" (Mark 1:2-3)

Mark is writing from an already-composed source rather than with a copy of Isaiah open in front of him; for he is apparently unaware that much of what he is quoting is not from Isaiah at all, but is in fact a merging of the first nine words of the Septuagint Greek version of Exodus 23:20 with a paraphrase of Hebrew Malachi 3:1, that is in turn joined with a paraphrase of Septuagint Isaiah 40:3:

> Here is my herald whom I send on ahead of you. (Mark 1:2)
> *Idou, apostello ton aggelon mou pro prosopou sou.*

This comes directly from Septuagint Exodus 23:20:

> *idou, ego apostello ton aggelon mou pro prosopou sou.*

But then Mark's source shifts to a paraphrase of Hebrew Malachi 3:1: "Look, I am sending my messenger who will clear a path before me." The "you" of Exodus is substituted for the "me" of Malachi, so that Mark's source can say that the messenger will "prepare your way." The Septuagint Greek version of Malachi 3:1 has "survey the way" (*epiblepsetai hodon*), so Mark's Greek is closer to the Hebrew "clear a path." Indeed, "clear a path" is the link in Mark's source to Isaiah 40:3, the origin, Mark thought, of the entire biblical passage he was citing:

> A voice crying aloud in the wilderness, "Prepare a way for the Lord; clear a straight path for him." (Mark 1:3)

Here Mark's Greek exactly reproduces the first thirteen words of Septuagint Isaiah 40:3 before becoming paraphrase at the end (Isaiah has "make straight the paths of our God," while Mark's source changes "our God" to "him.")

Clearly there was a long history behind this merging of various biblical texts and versions. Mark's source had already implicitly identified John the Baptist with Elijah on the basis of allusion to Septuagint IV Kings, where the prophet Elijah is described as "girt with a leather girdle about his loins" (*zōnēn dermatinēn periezōsmenos tēn osphyn autou*—IV Kings 1:8 LXX); for John is likewise described in Mark as dressed with a "leather belt around his waist" (*zōnēn dermatinēn peri tēn osphyn autou*—Mark 1:6). Early Christians had identified John the Baptist as Elijah-come-back on the basis of their interpretation of Malachi 4:5, which declares that the prophet Elijah will return "before the great and terrible day of the LORD comes," and since that day was thought to be imminent, John *must* have been Elijah. Such conclusions were drawn before Mark wrote his gospel, and he seems to be unaware of the richness of his source, as it merges a collection of allusions to the Hebrew and Greek Bibles. A complex pre-Markan tradition is visible here, one that left Aramaic-speaking first-generation Christianity far behind; Mark stands at least at the second remove from Peter and the third remove from Jesus—and more likely at the fourth remove, since his exact quotation of the first thirteen words of Septuagint Isaiah 40:3 (after the garbled merging of Exodus and Malachi that had been attributed to Isaiah) probably means that he is quoting from a written document that was itself based on oral tradition rather than directly from the unstable tradition itself.

Far from being an intimate of an intimate of Jesus, Mark wrote at the fourth remove from Jesus, dependent upon disconnected units of story, as is clear from his ignorance of the outline of Jesus' career. Beyond placing the Baptism at the beginning and the Crucifixion at the end, Mark relied for the rest on guesswork, though the point is perhaps better stated that Mark didn't care about the chronological outline of Jesus' ministry, since Mark's arrangement of units of story is thematic rather than chronological; they give the appearance of chronology only in that one follows the other, often strung together with one of Mark's favorite words, *euthus* ("immediately"). Moreover, as we shall see, that Matthew and Luke for the most part accept Mark's outline as historical tells us all we need to know about *their* distance from Jesus—one remove greater than Mark's, making them fifth removed!

That Mark's outline, up to chapter ten, is not historical is clear from the transitions between episodes; here is a selection of them as translated in the New English Bible:

Once he was approached by a leper (1:40)

When after some days (2:1)

Once more (2:13)

When Jesus was at table (2:15)

Once, when (2:18)

One Sabbath (2:23)

On another occasion (3:1)

On another occasion (4:1)

When he was alone (4:10)

That [same unspecified] day (4:35)

He left that place (6:1)

On one of his teaching journeys (6:6)

On another occasion (7:14)

There was another occasion about this time (8:1)

Jesus and his disciples set out (8:27)

On leaving those parts (10:1).

Moreover, Mark was as unfamiliar with Palestinian geography as he was with the outline of Jesus' career:

> They were now approaching Jerusalem, and when they reached Bethphage and Bethany, at the Mount of Olives, he sent two of his disciples…(Mark 11:1).

Anyone approaching Jerusalem from Jericho would come first to Bethany and then Bethphage, not the reverse. This is one of several passages showing that Mark knew little about Palestine; we must assume, Dennis Nineham argues, that "Mark did not know the relative positions of these two villages on the Jericho road" (1963, 294-295). Indeed, Mark knew so little about the area that he described Jesus going from Tyrian territory "by way of Sidon to the Sea of Galilee through the territory of the Ten Towns" (Mark 7:31); this is similar to saying that one goes from London to Paris by way of Edinburgh and Rome. The simplest assumption, says Nineham, is that "the Evangelist was not directly acquainted with Palestine" (40). Therefore, we may conclude that John Mark of Jerusalem is not our author.

So far we have uncovered only negative knowledge about the author of the Gospel of Mark: he was not from Palestine, was not an intimate of intimates of Jesus, and is as anonymous to us as he was to Luke. His knowledge of Jesus was based on material handed on to him from earlier generations. Where Mark stood in time and in his own scheme of history might be the best place to begin stating some positive knowledge about him.

At the beginning of his ninth chapter Mark has Jesus assure his disciples that "there are some of those standing here who will not taste death before they have seen the kingdom of God already come in power." And in the thirteenth chapter Mark has Jesus declare that after the destruction of the Jerusalem temple ("Not one stone will be left upon another"—13:2), there will come a period of great distress on Earth and disorder in the heavens, followed immediately by Jesus' Second Coming:

> But in those days, after that distress, the sun will be darkened, the moon will not give her light; the stars will come falling from the sky, the celestial powers will be shaken. Then they will see the Son of Man coming in the clouds with great power and glory…In the same way, when you see all this happening, you may know that the end is near, at the very

I: Who Wrote the Gospel of Mark?

door. I tell you this, the present generation will live to see it all. (Mark 13:24-26, 29-30)

Mark writes for an audience that knows about the destruction of the Jerusalem temple in 70 C.E. and both accepts it as a foreshadowing of the apocalypse and wonders why that event did not happen immediately. He is clearly speaking to an audience that is not acquainted with any eyewitnesses of Jesus but believes that a few such must still be alive. Since the cosmic disorder and the Second Coming were still in Mark's future, and since a contemporary of Jesus would have been about seventy-five years old when Jerusalem was destroyed by the Romans in the year 70 and there must have been very few of those contemporaries left, we can readily get Mark's point. Mark himself clearly did not know any eyewitnesses of Jesus, or they might have corrected his gospel for him; so it is not hard to date the Gospel of Mark shortly after 70 C.E., and place it outside Palestine. Nor is it hard to grasp that Mark's Gospel expresses a misguided Christian apocalypticism, since the Son of Man did not appear in the clouds before the end of the first Christian generation. And indeed the "delay of the *Parousia*" (as Jesus' failure to return has come to be called) is one of the main reasons for Matthew's and Luke's need to produce revised versions of Mark, correcting this and other problems in the earlier gospel, as we shall see below.

Indeed it might be possible to date Mark more precisely than "shortly after 70"; we might be able to name the year, within a margin of error of two. I say this on the basis of Mark's use of the Book of Daniel in his thirteenth chapter, where he has Jesus explain that the Jewish war with Rome that culminated in the temple's destruction in 70 was not itself the motive for the Second Coming of the Son of Man:

When you hear the noise of battle near at hand and news of battles far away, do not be alarmed. Such things are bound to happen; but the end is still to come.

There will be war, earthquakes, and famines: "With these things the birth-pangs of the new age begin." Christians will be persecuted and "summoned to appear before governors and kings" (Mark is aware of the career of Paul):

> But when you see the "abomination of desolation" usurping a place which is not his (let the reader understand), then those who are in Judaea must take to the hills. (Mark 13:8-10,14)

"Let the reader understand" is Mark's hint of a prophetic allusion to the last chapter of the Book of Daniel:

> I said to the man clothed in linen who was above the waters of the river, "How long will it be before these portents cease?"…"It shall be for a time, times and a half. When the power of the holy people ceases to be dispersed, all these things shall come to an end." I heard but did not understand, and so I said, "Sir, what will the issue of these things be?" He replied, "Go your way, Daniel, for the words are kept secret and sealed till the time of the end…From the time when the regular offering [in the temple] is abolished and the "abomination of desolation" is set up, there shall be an interval of one thousand two hundred and ninety days." (Dan. 12:6-9,11)

So Daniel's "time, times, and half a time" is three and a half years, or twelve hundred and ninety days. The author of Daniel was referring, with the "abomination of desolation," to the altar to Zeus that Antiochus IV established in the Jerusalem temple in December, 167 B.C.E., as I Maccabees 1:54 tells us. But in Mark's eyes, Daniel really was speaking of Mark's own time, the "time of the end," when *another* "abomination of desolation" was set up in the Jerusalem temple. For according to Josephus, the regular offering ceased in the temple in July, 70, the temple was burnt in August, and later that month the imperial Roman eagle was set up in the temple precincts and sacrifice was offered to it; then in September the temple was razed to the ground (Josephus, *The Jewish War*, Chapters 6, 7). Three and a half years thereafter would be early in the year 74. Mark was written during that interval, sometime in 71-73, and its author expected the Second Coming of the Son of Man in 74. It should not be surprising that a first-century author might apply the Book of Daniel to the Jewish War; Josephus himself did so, he tells us, in the summer of the year 70, at the height of the siege (Josephus, 309).

That Mark wrote shortly after 70 rather than a few years before, as some have argued, is further evidenced, in my view, in his thirteenth chapter. Mark knows about some messianic pretenders who misled early Christians:

I: Who Wrote the Gospel of Mark?

> Then, if anyone says to you, "Look, here is the Messiah," or "Look, there he is," do not believe it. Imposters will come claiming to be messiahs or prophets, and they will produce signs and wonders to mislead God's chosen, if such a thing were possible. (Mark 13:21-22)

Josephus tells us about Menahem son of Judas (died 66 C.E.) and Simon son of Gioras (died 70 C.E.), both of whom were striking messianic pretenders (Josephus, 157-159, 370-372). The false messiahs of Mark 13:21 were to appear "then," that is, during the "great distress":

> For those days will bring distress such as has never been until now since the beginning of the world which God created—and will never be again. If the Lord had not cut short that time of troubles, no living thing could survive. However, for the sake of his own, whom he has chosen, he has cut short the time. (Mark 13:19-21)

As far as Mark was concerned the Jewish War was over; there remained only the cosmic disorder and the Second Coming.

So Mark was an apocalyptic Christian who mistakenly expected the Second Coming in 74 and who wrote a year or two before that date, living outside Palestine but not too far outside (the noise of battle was "near at hand"—13:7). Moreover, Mark wrote in a not very literate *koine* Greek and knew Jesus' language of Aramaic, quoting several of Jesus' sayings in Greek letters transliterated from that language. This kind of bilingualism leads some scholars to place Mark's origin in "Syria, where Greek was the common language, but where a substratum of Aramaic seems to have survived" (Kee, 1977, 149).

So perhaps in "small-town southern Syria" (Kee, 105) in the early seventies, a Greek-speaking non-Jewish Christian wrote about Jesus for an audience like himself of non-Jewish Christians who mistakenly expected that the destruction of Jerusalem was the beginning of the end of the age. That Mark and his audience *were* non-Jewish is clear from chapter seven, where Mark knows just enough about Jewish customs to get them wrong as he tries to explain them to his readers:

> [S]ome of his followers were eating their food with "defiled" hands—in other words without washing them. (For the Pharisees and the Jews in general never eat without

washing the hands, in obedience to an old established tradition; and on coming from the marketplace they never eat without first washing.) (Mark 7:2-4)

But in fact, "the evidence of the *Talmud* is that in the time of Jesus ritual washing of hands before meals was obligatory only on the priests" (Nineham, 1963, 193). Mark was confusing Jewish practice of his own time with Palestinian practice of forty years before. And as for Mark's notion that "on coming from the marketplace they never eat without first washing," "all efforts to prove this a custom even of the strictest Jews must fail" (Nineham, 194, quoting the Jewish authority A. Buechler). Not only was Mark non-Jewish, he seems to have been an adult convert to Christianity, for he clearly did not grow up with the Scriptures in his hands. He frequently seems unaware that his source is quoting or paraphrasing the Old Testament, and when his source misquotes Scripture, he fails to correct the error.

Most of the references to the Old Testament in the Gospel of Mark come from within Mark's sources rather than from the hand of Mark himself, and he treats such references uncritically. In the story of the Rich Young Ruler, for example, Mark's source has Jesus misquote the Decalogue:

You know the commandments: "Do not murder; do not commit adultery; do not steal; do not give false evidence; do not defraud; honor your father and mother." (Mark 10:19)

Mark's source invents a new commandment ("defraud"). Both Matthew (16:18) and Luke (18:20) silently drop "defraud," assuming that Jesus would certainly know the Ten Commandments.

Mark's failure to check his sources sometimes involves him in genuine historical error, as in the Sabbath controversy in chapter two. When the Pharisees object that Jesus' followers, by plucking grain on the Sabbath, do "what is forbidden," Jesus replies:

Have you never read what David did when he and his men were hungry and had nothing to eat? He went into the house of God, in the time of Abiathar the High Priest, and ate the sacred bread, though no one but a priest is allowed to eat it. (Mark 2:25-26)

Actually, Ahimelech was high priest at the time (I Sam. 21:1-6);

Abiathar was his son. No scholar of the Bible, Mark let this piece of mis-information slip into his gospel unchecked. Both Matthew (12:3) and Luke (6:4) silently correct Mark's error.

Mark's uncritical use of his sources' biblical references relates directly to his misunderstanding of Jesus' parables and their purpose. After Mark's account of Jesus' parable of the sower and the seed, his disciples "questioned him about the parables":

> He replied, "To you the secret of the kingdom of God has been given; but to those who are outside everything comes by way of parables, so that they may look and look, but see nothing; they may hear and hear, but understand nothing; otherwise they might turn to God and be forgiven." (Mark 4:10-12)

Mark seems unaware that verse 12 is a paraphrase of Isaiah 6:9-10, taking the statement from his source at face value that Jesus spoke in parables to ensure that the un-elect ("those…outside") would be unable to "turn to God and be forgiven." Mark saw Christianity as a mystery cult, a secret knowledge given only to the elect. Had he known Isaiah chapter six and its context—as Matthew, using Mark as his source, clearly did—had he, like Matthew, checked the ultimate source of his source, Mark might have told this story in something like the way Matthew did:

> It has been granted to you to know the secrets [plural] of the kingdom of Heaven; but to those others it has not been granted. For the man who has will be given more, and the man who has not will forfeit even what he has. That is why I speak to them in parables; for they look without seeing, and listen without understanding. For there is a prophecy of Isaiah which is being fulfilled for them: "You may hear and hear, but you will never understand; you may look and look, but you will never see. For this people's mind has become gross; their ears are dulled, and their eyes closed. Otherwise, their eyes might see, their ears hear, and their mind understand, and then they might turn again, and I would heal them." (Matt.13:11-15)

In Matthew's view, Jesus spoke in parables to clarify his message, not obscure it. Matthew saw that Mark was paraphrasing Isaiah, went back to the original, and quoted it from the Septuagint, having grasped that Isaiah supported this own more sensible view of Jesus' reasons for speaking in parables.

Mark's view of Jesus' parables is not simply a mistake, however, it is part of a central theme in his gospel, a considered argument rather than a blunder. For unlike the other evangelists, Mark held that essential to the "secret of the kingdom of God" is what Wilhelm Wrede has called the "Messianic Secret" (in his classic 1901 work that appeared in English translation in 1971 under this title). According to Mark, among fellow Jews Jesus insisted on hiding his identity, right up until Passion Week. When Peter, for example, grasped as early as chapter eight that "You are the Messiah," Jesus "gave them strict orders not to tell anyone about him" (8:30). And that Jesus gave the same order to many he encountered is a central theme in Mark (1:24; 1:34; 1:44; 3:12; 5:43; 8:30 and elsewhere), one that is very difficult to understand.

The idea seems to be Mark's invention, and scarcely seems to belong in the stories of Jesus' activities that Mark has gathered from Christian tradition. In chapter five, for example, Jesus is shown raising from death the daughter of Jairus, in a household whose inhabitants laugh at him for declaring that "the child is not dead; she is asleep." He enters the dead girl's room and tells her to "Get up." And when the child "got up and walked about...they were beside themselves with amazement. He gave them strict orders to let no one hear about it" (Mark 5:42-43). Clearly such an act, had it actually happened, would be impossible to hide; Jesus' demand seems nonsensical. The demand fits with Mark's theme of the Messianic Secret but not in its context in a traditional miracle story. Mark is imposing the theme on material he has inherited and that is quite resistant to that theme. But Mark's editorial activity is deliberate; for him there really is a "secret of the kingdom of God." For Mark, the *real* Messianic Secret is that, contrary to the popular understanding, the job of the Messiah is not to rule at first, but first to suffer and die before returning to rule. Mark combined the political ideal of the Messiah, widely popular and devoutly wished for in first-century Palestine (as Josephus attests, and based on such biblical passages as Isaiah 11 and Daniel 7 where the "son of man" will come on the clouds to assume kingly power), with Second Isaiah's concept of the Suffering Servant. A concept of the Messiah "pierced for our transgressions, tortured for our iniquities," by whose "scourging we are healed" (Isa. 53:5), was a concept so radical, in Mark's view, that not even the disciples, not even Peter, understood it:

> "And you," he asked, "who do you say that I am?" Peter replied: "You are the Messiah." Then he gave them strict orders not to tell anyone about him; and he began to teach them that the Son of Man had to undergo great sufferings, and to be rejected by the elders, chief priests, and doctors of the law; to be put to death, and to rise again three days afterwards. He spoke about it plainly. At this Peter took him by the arm and began to rebuke him. (Mark 8:29-32)

The Messianic Secret is the "central theological idea pervading the entire Gospel [of Mark] and which concretely determines its structure" (Conzelmann and Lindemann, 1988, 219). We have to attribute this idea to Mark and not to his sources, for it looks like a deliberate misunderstanding of those sources.

"Misunderstanding" isn't the right word, of course; for though Mark is uncritical of his sources' use of Scripture, he is not uncritical of their interpretation of Jesus. The theme of the Messianic Secret is an obsession with Mark, demanding that he change his sources. We have already seen this happening with regard to the parables and miracles of Jesus. To use a current idiom, Mark has deconstructed those sources, undermining their presentations of Jesus as the teacher of wisdom (in parables) and wonder-working divine man (in miracles). To Mark, these presentations do not adequately interpret Jesus' Messiahship, so he makes the teacher teach in order *not* to teach but to obscure; and he has the divine man demand secrecy for his acts of power in order to show that his real power is his self-giving powerlessness on the cross. Nobody understood him; only Mark has got the point.

The Messianic Secret continues even in Mark's resurrection story; the Resurrection remains as secret as the Messiahship. Only the three women at the tomb are told about it, and "They said nothing to anybody, for they were afraid" (Mark 16:8)—the last words in the Gospel of

Mark, according to the oldest and best manuscripts. This is very puzzling, but we must accept it as Mark's deliberate intention. We need to take quite seriously the statement to the women at the tomb: "He has been raised again; he is not here" (16:6), and Jesus' statement at the Last Supper: "never again shall I drink from the fruit of the vine until that day when I drink it new in the kingdom of God" (14:25). For Mark, Jesus really is "not here" for the forty-four years that were to lapse between Resurrection and *Parousia* (30-74 C.E.); for Mark, the Resurrection *was* the ascension; "He has been raised again" *really* meant "he is not here." Jesus is the secret Messiah before the Crucifixion and will come from heaven as Son of Man at the *Parousia*; but there is no more role for him on Earth until that time. And even the Resurrection is part of the Messianic Secret, fully understood only now in the writing of the Gospel of Mark, two or three years before the *Parousia*. The last verse of Mark has been a puzzle to many (that the women "said nothing to anyone"), a puzzle even to Matthew and Luke, who dropped that last verse and presented the women going to the disciples and telling their glad news; they even added Resurrection-appearance stories to prove their point. But for the author of Mark the conclusion was apt because it merely continued his theme of the Messianic Secret.

That there are no Resurrection-appearance stories in Mark's Gospel, however, does not mean that this author did not know any; he knew at least two of them and used them in his Gospel, deconstructing them as Resurrection appearances and back-dating them as events in the earthly career of Jesus: we know them now as the voice from heaven at the baptism, and the Transfiguration.

The first of these had a long history in Christian tradition before Mark: "Thou art my son, my Beloved; on thee my favor rests" (Mark 1:11). This statement is a merging of Psalm 2:7 ("Thou art my son") with a widely-used oral-tradition version of Isaiah 42:1; we know that the latter is the case because Matthew cites the Isaiah passage in this form in another context (not the baptism): "Here is my servant whom I have chosen, my beloved, on whom my favor rests; I will put my Spirit upon him" (Matt. 12:18). But in Christian tradition before Mark, Ps. 2:7 had long been applied to Jesus only as a Resurrection saying, since already in the fifties and perhaps sooner. Paul wrote to the Romans that Jesus was "declared Son of God by a mighty act in that he rose from the dead" (Romans 1:4). In Acts Luke makes explicit the biblical reference Paul had in mind, showing him preaching at Pisidian Antioch "the good news that God, who made the promise to the fathers, has fulfilled it for the children by raising Jesus from the dead, as indeed it stands written, in the second Psalm: 'You are my son; this day I have begotten you'" (Acts 13:32-33). Mark's source had already combined Ps. 2:7 with the Isaiah passage as Matthew knew it ("my beloved, on whom my favor rests; I will put my Spirit upon him"); but since in Mark's view the passage from Ps. 2:7 had to be deconstructed as part of a Resurrection story, and since he wanted to present the Spirit coming upon Jesus at the baptism, he turns the whole saying into a voice from heaven at that time, changing "I will put my Spirit upon him" into the famous narrative of the dove descending from the sky upon Jesus. That the narrative is the invention of Mark is shown by its ineptness. For the Greek phrase "my Spirit" (*to pneuma mou*) becomes in Mark "the spirit" (*to pneuma*—1: 10), a phrase embarrassing to both Matthew and Luke when they used Mark's baptism scene. "In Jewish literature it is unheard of to speak of 'the Spirit'...when the spirit of God is meant, [for] the simple word 'spirit' would much rather be taken to mean a demon or the wind" (Bultmann, 1976, 251). This is why Matthew changes Mark's "the Spirit" to "the spirit of God" (Matt. 3:16) and Luke changes it to "the Holy Spirit" (Luke 3:22). So Psalm 2:7, taken in pre-Markan tradition as a statement to Jesus at his Resurrection certifying his divine sonship, becomes in Mark's hands, combined with Isa. 42:1-2, a statement from heaven at Jesus' baptism—Mark's truly creative use of his source, and one very troubling to those who in turn used Mark as a source.

Like the voice from heaven at Jesus' baptism, the Transfiguration scene in Mark also began in Christian tradition as a Resurrection-appearance narrative. This has long been suspected (Bultmann, 1976, 259; Koester, 237). Recently, some have suggested that another Resurrection narrative, that found in the apocryphal Gospel of Peter, used the same source that Mark employed in his Transfiguration story: Mark's Transfiguration "may indeed be nothing else but a faint echo of the account which the *Gospel of Peter* has preserved in full" (Koester, 1990, 238). Mark chose not to present Resurrection appearances in his gospel because he held that the next time Jesus would be seen after his resurrection was at the Second Coming, now only a year or two in Mark's future, as he saw it. But he possessed a powerful Resurrection-appearance story and he didn't want to waste it, so he deconstructed it and back-dated it into the earthly career of Jesus as the Transfiguration, an account that Matthew could not understand:

> Six days later, Jesus took Peter, James and John with him and led them up to a high mountain where they were alone; and in their presence he was transfigured; his clothes became dazzling white, with a whiteness no bleacher on earth could equal…Then a cloud appeared, casting its shadow over them, and out of the cloud came a voice: "This is my Son, my Beloved; listen to him." (Mark 9:2-7)

In Christian tradition before Mark this scene was recounted as a post-Resurrection divine certification of Jesus as Son of God, as we have seen from Acts and from Paul's Letter to the Romans. As Mark found it in the tradition, the divine voice was a blending of Ps. 2:7 ("my son") with Isa. 42:1 ("my beloved") and Deut. 18:15 ("listen to him"). This last passage from Deuteronomy had, in Christian interpretation, seen Jesus as the new prophet like Moses: "The LORD your God will raise up a prophet from among you like myself [says Moses], and you shall *listen to him.*" In Mark's source, the voice from heaven may have introduced post-Resurrection sayings by Jesus which Mark in turn back-dated into his gospel, but this is speculative. Certainly Mark uses the Transfiguration story to certify Jesus' divine sonship before the Crucifixion rather than after the Resurrection, though even this certification must remain under the compulsion of the Messianic Secret:

> On their way down the mountain, he enjoined them not to tell anyone what they had seen until the Son of Man had risen from the dead. They seized upon these words, and discussed among themselves what this "rising from the dead" could mean. (Mark 9:9-10)

The disciples in Mark fail to understand the Messianic Secret; so do all until Mark writes his gospel, just before the *Parousia*, to make it clear. Indeed, Matthew couldn't understand Mark's story either (not knowing it was a deconstructed Resurrection appearance), so he deconstructed it again, reducing it from literal experience to "a vision" (Matt. 17:9) and eliminating the disciples' inability to understand "this rising from the dead," for the doctrine of the Resurrection had been standard Hasidic and Pharasaic teaching for two centuries, as any first-generation Jewish Christian would have known despite what Mark implies.

Mark's theme of the Messianic Secret controls even his presentation of the disciples' thought-processes. I think the ultimate source of Mark's strange theme is the Book of Daniel, especially the twelfth chapter, which underlies Mark's apocalyptic thirteenth chapter, as I demonstrated above. There in Daniel, Mark found a "secret" that was "sealed until the time of the end" (Dan. 12:4). "None...shall understand" that secret; "only the wise leaders shall understand" (Dan. 12:10). Mark saw himself in that role, revealing the (Messianic) secret in his own time, for him the "time of the end," during that three-and-a-half-year interval between "the time when the regular offering is abolished and the 'abomination of desolation' is set up" (Dan. 12:11) (both of which happened, as Mark read Daniel, in the year 70 C.E.), and the "end of the age" (Dan. 12:13), which Mark expected in 74:

> [T]he words are kept secret and sealed until the time of the end. Many shall purify themselves and be refined, making themselves shining white, but the wicked shall continue in wickedness and none of them shall understand; only the wise leaders shall understand. From the time when the regular offering is abolished and the "abomination of desolation" is set up, there shall be an interval of one thousand two hundred and ninety days. Happy the man who waits and lives to see the completion of one thousand three hundred and thirty-five days! But go your way to the end and rest, and you shall rise to your destiny at the end of the age. (Dan. 12:10-13)

Why the Book of Daniel should be so important to Mark will become clear in the next chapter.

MARK'S APOCALYPTIC MIND

CENTRAL TO THE GOSPEL of Mark is its insistence that those who saw Jesus in the flesh would also see him come again as the Son of Man: "He also said, 'I tell you this: there are some of those standing here who will not taste death before they have seen the kingdom of God already come in power'" (Mark 9:1). This spectacularly wrong prediction has puzzled readers ever since. Mark is quite clear about his expectations; when the High Priest of Israel asks Jesus on the night of his arrest, "Are you the Messiah?" Mark has Jesus answer, "I am; and you [plural] will see the Son of Man seated at the right hand of the Power and coming with the clouds of heaven" (Mark 14:62). Mark is of course alluding to the apocalyptic vision in Daniel chapter 7: "I saw one like a son of man coming with the clouds of heaven;...sovereignty and glory and kingly power were given to him" (Dan. 7:13-14). Mark believed that Daniel's vision was going to come true in his own time, that contemporaries of this same High Priest would see the Son of Man. Mark, that is, shared in a common illusion of his time, that an ineluctable future is divinely revealed to us; we are, like Oedipus, fated to endure what heaven has foreseen. To learn what he took to be the foreordained meaning of his own time, Mark went to the Book of Daniel, believing that it correctly predicted events of the 70s C.E.

It is not too much to say that a key to the mind of Mark lies in the Book of Daniel, for Mark was the first Christian writer to use that book in an effort to understand the implications of the destruction of Jerusalem's temple by a Roman army in 70 C.E. In the chapter before Jesus' interrogation by the High Priest, Mark has Jesus declare that the temple would be "thrown down," "not one stone...left upon another"; for the "abomination of desolation" would be set up, and then, after that distress, the sun will be darkened, the moon will not give her light; the stars will come falling from the sky, the celestial powers will be shaken. Then they will see the Son of Man coming in the clouds with great power and glory. (Mark 13:2,14,24-25)

Just as Mark found the "son of man" in Daniel 7:13, he found the "abomination of desolation" in Daniel 12:11, and read those passages as applying to his own time. Now it is not that Mark misused the Book of Daniel by reading it as predictive of its own future; for Daniel itself insists that it is about "days far ahead" (8:26), "the end of this age" (2:28), when the "God of heaven will establish a kingdom" (2:44). Rather it was the apocalyptic author of the Book of Daniel who abused his readers with self-disconfirming predictions requiring endless re-interpretation. This abuse takes a specific form: as S. B. Frost has said, the Book of Daniel "is a dishonest production, which, although in the Bible, claims to be in fact what it is not" (*IDB*, I, 766).

The Book of Daniel presents itself as having been written in the sixth century B.C.E., during the reigns of the Babylonian rulers Nebuchadnezzar and Belshazzar and the Persians Cyrus and Darius. From that point in time it presents itself as predicting events in the ancient Near East during the fifth, fourth, third, and second centuries B.C.E. But strangely, whenever Daniel talks about the sixth century it is vague and inaccurate, and when it talks about the second century it is quite detailed and exact. This gives us a clue as to its actual time of writing. With regard to the sixth century B.C.E., the book opens by declaring:

In the third year of the reign of Jehoiakim king of Judah, Nebuchadnezzar king of Babylon came to Jerusalem and laid siege to it. The Lord delivered Jehoiakim king of Judah into his power, together with all that was left of the vessels of the house of God; and he carried them off to the land of Shinar. (1:1-2)

But in fact Jehoiakim reigned for eleven years; it was only in the first year of his son and successor Jehoiachin that Nebuchadnezzar laid siege to Jerusalem, captured it, and "carried off all the treasures of the house of the LORD" (see II Kings 28:8-13). The author of Daniel is quite weak on his facts about the sixth century B.C.E., and continues to be so in his account of the fall of Babylon to Persia in the year 539. He writes that "Belshazzar king of the Chaldaeans was slain, and Darius the Mede took the kingdom" (Dan. 5:30). But of course it was Cyrus the Persian who conquered Babylon (see Ezra 1:1); there never was a King Darius the Mede. The author of Daniel confusedly imagines him in place of Darius the Persian, who succeeded Cyrus' son Cambyses in 521 B.C.E. The author of Daniel also confusedly imagines that Cyrus succeeded Darius (though Darius in fact succeeded Cyrus' son), and imagines that Belshazzar was the son of Nebuchadnezzar (5:11), though he was in fact the son of Nabonidus (see *ABD* IV, 973). Nabonidus, in turn, was "not related to any of his predecessors" (*ABD*, IV, 973), including Nebuchadnezzar; so the author of the Book of Daniel was ignorant even of the lineage of the ruler, Belshazzar, in whose court Daniel was said to be "chief of the magicians" (5:11). Thus it ought not surprise the attentive reader of the Book of Daniel that modern critical scholars of the Bible are unanimous in their conviction that Daniel "actually comes from the 2nd century B.C.E." (*ABD* II, 33) and that its pretense of coming from the sixth century is a literary fiction intended to impress its readers with the supposed accuracy of its foreknowledge of the next several hundred years. Mark, of course, did not have the advantage of knowing this, and fell for Daniel's pretense of genuinely predicting its own—and, Mark thought, his own—future. To read Mark aright, we must first read Daniel.

Mark was not the first biblical writer to interpret the Book of Daniel; that honor goes to one who preceded Mark by about a hundred and seventy years, the anonymous author of First Maccabees, who tells about the Maccabean War against Antiochus IV of Syria in the 160s B.C.E. Being close to the events described in the Book of Daniel, this writer saw clearly that Daniel really did concern the 160s B.C.E.; in fact, First Maccabees can give us information necessary to understand Daniel. Written about 100 B.C.E. (*ABD* IV, 441), I Maccabees mentions the story of "Hananiah, Azariah, and Mishael" (the three Hebrews thrown into the fiery furnace in Daniel chapter three), and notes that "Daniel was a man of faith, and he was rescued from the lion's jaws" (I Macc. 2:59-60). Having obviously read

---

SIX TYPICAL FEATURES OF APOCALYPTIC LITERATURE

1. ESCHATOLOGICAL: Authors of apocalyptic believe they are living in the last days (from Greek *eschaton*, "last, utmost").

2. PSEUDEPIGRAPHIC: Apocalyptic works usually present themselves as having been written by religious heroes of the past, such as Enoch, Ezra, or Daniel, who "predict" the future (i.e., the past and present of the actual author).

3. VISIONARY: Presented as a series of visions seen and reported by the religious hero, and then interpreted by a heavenly being.

4. LITERARY AND ALLUSIVE: The "visions" are fictional, dependent on earlier works. Daniel alludes to Jeremiah, Revelation and Second Esdras to Daniel.

5. ALWAYS WRONG: End-time prediction is necessarily self-disconfirming, and thus apocalyptic is usually revisionist.

6. REVISIONIST: Wrong predictions must be re-interpreted by a later generation of apocalyptic believers. Daniel re-interprets Jeremiah, Mark and Second Esdras re-interpret Daniel, Matthew re-interprets Mark.

---

the Book of Daniel, the author of I Maccabees also understood what it meant by the "abomination of desolation" set up by the "king of the north" who would send "armed forces" to "desecrate the the sanctuary and the citadel and do away with the regular offering" (Dan. 11:31). He uses the same terms to describe the actions of the agents of Antiochus IV in Judaea in 167 B.C.E.:

> [T]he king sent agents with written orders to Jerusalem...Burnt offerings, sacrifices, and libations in the temple were forbidden; sabbaths and feast-days were to be profaned; the temple and its ministers to be defiled...On the fifteenth day of the month Kislev in the [Seleucid calendar] year 145 [167 B.C.E.], "the abomination of desolation" was set up on the altar. (I Macc. 1:44-45,54)

II: Mark's Apocalyptic Mind

Antiochus had ordered the establishment of an altar to Zeus in Jerusalem's temple, a desecration that soon evoked a rebellion, the Maccabean War described in I Maccabees, which quotes the Book of Daniel to describe its beginnings. First Maccabees is the only biblical book that shows any historical understanding of apocalyptic literature like Daniel; not until the modern period of critical study of the Bible did such understanding begin to dawn again.

Along with the Book of Revelation, Daniel is one of the two "apocalyptic" books in the Bible, a literary form that takes its name from the first word in Revelation, *Apocalypsis* ("a disclosure, a revelation"). Apocalyptic books generally contain a series of visions, related in the first person, and speeches interpretive of such visions. The interpreter is usually a heavenly figure—in Daniel, the angel Gabriel—who reveals that the visions are about the future:

> In my visions of the night, I, Daniel, was gazing intently and saw a great sea. (Dan. 7:13)
>
> "I have come [says Gabriel] to explain to you what will happen to your people in days to come; for this too is a vision for those days." (Dan. 10:14)

Since the Book of Revelation was written after Mark, it will not figure here in an account of Mark's apocalyptic mind; Daniel, on the other hand, exercised a powerful influence on that mind.

The first thing to grasp about the apocalyptic mind is that it is delusional; it has a distorted view of the world (that the apocalypt's own time is the end time) and a distressingly amoral value system (that in the destruction soon to come, all will die horribly except the apocalypt and his peer group). Time and again we read that "the vision points to the time of the end" (Dan. 7:17), when the enemy of the "faithful" will "meet his end with no one to help him" (Dan. 11:45). The apocalyptic mind feeds on the revenge soon to come "at the end of this age" when "distress such as has never been" will visit the earth (Dan. 12:1, 13).

Though full-blown apocalypticism is relatively rare in the Bible, achieving full literary form only in Daniel and Revelation, elements of apocalypticism mar much of the New Testament, a burden Christianity is still unable to overcome. Apocalypticism is fortunately rare because it is, in the words of Paul Hanson, a mentality of "alienation and crisis" (1987, 75), a brooding and vengeful response to social or cultural calamity. The Book of Daniel responds to the efforts, in the 160s B.C.E., of the Syrian King Antiochus IV to stamp out Judaism in his vassal territory of Judaea and replace it with the "superior" religion and culture of Hellenism; Mark's apocalypticism stems from the terrible destruction of Jerusalem by the Romans in 70 C.E. and the persecution of Christians in Mark's area (perhaps Syria) attendant upon the Jewish war with Rome.

Careful readers of the Bible have determined that the Book of Daniel was written in the second century B.C.E. despite its claim of being four centuries older, because it clearly really is about that second century, a period it regards as the "time of the end" (Dan. 11:40). The fictive author, "Daniel," is told to "seal the book until the time of the end" (12:4); that the Book of Daniel was promulgated just before the middle of the second century B.C.E. (and already influenced the author of I Maccabees about 100 B.C.E., as we saw), makes it clear that those who promulgated it regarded their time as that "time of the end" and wanted Daniel to stamp their interpretation on it. Each of Daniel's visions is interpreted in the text of the book as referring to the days when "your people will be delivered" after a "time of distress" (12:1), a time when "the God of heaven will establish a kingdom" (2:44). And each vision culminates, as its interpretation in the text shows, in the 160s B.C.E., the "time of the end" in the eyes of the author of Daniel. That he was wrong meant that his book would have to be re-interpreted, the constant fate of all self-disconfirming prediction; Mark's re-interpretation applied Daniel not to the second century B.C.E. but to the first century of our own era.

The first vision of the "future" in the Book of Daniel is Nebuchadnezzar's dream in chapter two, a vision that concerns "what is to be at the end of this age" (2:28). Daniel both describes and interprets the dream:

[Y]ou saw a great image…The head of the image was of fine gold, its breast and arms of silver, its belly and thighs of bronze, its legs of iron, its feet part iron and part clay. (Dan. 2:31-35)

II: Mark's Apocalyptic Mind

Daniel's interpretation follows:

> [Y]ou [Nebuchadnezzar] are that head of gold. After you there shall arise another king-
> dom, inferior to yours, and yet a third kingdom...And there shall be a fourth kingdom,
> strong as iron,...it shall break and shatter the whole earth. As, in your vision, the feet and
> toes were part potter's clay and part iron, it shall be a divided kingdom...In the period
> of those kings the God of heaven will establish a kingdom. (Dan. 2:38-44)

Daniel's interpretation to the king is clear: the Babylonian empire (gold) will be succeeded by Darius' Median empire (silver; see Dan. 5:31), by the Persian empire of Cyrus (bronze; see Dan. 10:1), and by the Greek empire of Alexander the Great (iron) that conquered the Persians and the "whole earth" but became a "divided kingdom." (On Alexander's early death his empire was parceled among his generals, Seleucus getting the part that concerned the author of Daniel—Syria and Palestine.) Seleucus established the "Seleucid" dynasty, being succeeded by his heirs Antiochus I (died 261 B.C.E.), Antiochus II (d. 246), Seleucus II (d. 225), Antiochus III (d. 187), Seleucus IV (d. 175), Antiochus IV (d. 164), and then others not mentioned in the Book of Daniel. That the last deeds of Antiochus IV are described as happening "At the time of the end" (Dan. 11:40) and that this king was in fact succeeded by nine others of the same name (the last being Antiochus XIII, whose reign ended in 64 B.C.E.) is one more clear indication of the date of the Book of Daniel. Still, chapter two of Daniel does not specify which of "those kings" will see the God of heaven perform this mighty act; for that, we must go to Daniel's own visions in chapters seven through eleven, each of which again describes a historical sequence culminating in the first half of the second century B.C.E.

In his first vision, Daniel sees "four huge beasts coming up out of the sea" (7:3), one "like a lion," a second "like a bear," a third "like a leopard with four birds' wings on its back," and a fourth, "dreadful and grisly," with "ten horns," among them a "little horn" that "spoke proud words."

> Then because of the proud words that the horn was speaking, I went on watching until
> the beast was killed and its carcass destroyed...I was still watching in visions of the night

and I saw one like a son of man coming with the clouds of heaven...Sovereignty and glory and kingly power were given to him. (Dan. 7:11-13)

A heavenly figure then interprets this puzzling vision for Daniel:

"These great beasts, four in number," he said, "are four kingdoms which shall rise from the ground. But the saints of the Most High shall receive the kingly power." (Dan. 7:17)

But Daniel remains unsatisfied, wanting to know "what the fourth beast meant," and especially who was the little horn "speaking proud words," since in his vision he saw it "waging war with the saints and overcoming them" (Dan. 7:22). In other words, the point of this episode is the identity of that figure. So Daniel is told that the "little horn"

shall hurl defiance at the Most High. He shall plan to alter the customary times and law; and the saints shall be delivered into his power for a time and times and half a time. Then the court shall sit, and he shall be deprived of his sovereignty, and greatness of all the kingdoms under heaven shall be given to the people of the saints of the Most High. Their kingly power is an everlasting power. (Dan. 7:25-27)

Much of this explanation is cryptic, and it is not at all clear in this context what "time and times and half a time" means, though the allusion to Antiochus IV and his attack upon Judaism seems clear enough. But the vision needs more explanation, and the Book of Daniel supplies this in the form of yet another vision and its interpretation, one that leaves no doubt about its meaning, since the angel Gabriel himself makes it clear, naming the empires depicted in it. Daniel's next vision occurred, we are told, two years later, and was one "similar to my former vision" (8:2). This time he sees a "ram with two horns"; then a "he-goat" with a "prominent horn between its eyes," "skimming over the whole earth." He sees it "strike the ram" "to the ground." But then the he-goat's "great horn snapped and in its place there sprang out towards the four quarters of heaven four prominent horns."

Out of one of them there issued one small horn, which made a prodigious show of strength south and east and towards the fairest of all lands. It aspired to be as great as the

> host of heaven…It aspired to be as great as the Prince of the host, suppressed his regu-
> lar offering and even threw down his sanctuary. (Dan. 8:3, 5, 7, 8-11)

Daniel, "trying to understand" the vision, is approached by Gabriel, who explains that "the vision points to the time of the end," and that the ram "signifies the kings of Media and Persia," the "he-goat is the kingdom of the Greeks and the great horn on his forehead is the first king."

> As for the horn which was snapped off and replaced by four horns: four kingdoms shall
> rise out of that nation, but not with power comparable to his. In the last days of those
> kingdoms, when their sin is at its height, a king shall appear, harsh and grim, a master of
> stratagem…He shall work havoc among great nations and upon a holy people…He
> shall challenge even the Prince of princes and be broken, but not by human hands.
> (Dan. 8:20-25)

We could not find a clearer symbolic account of Alexander's defeat of the Persian empire, his early death and the division of his conquests among his four generals—Cassander, Lysimachus, Ptolemy and Seleucus—and the effort of the descendant of Seleucus (Antiochus IV) to destroy Judaism. But note that the vision also predicts that Antiochus will be "broken" by superhuman means, though the process remains vague. The author of Daniel still has more predicting to do in the remaining visions that complete his book.

Daniel's next chapter drops the device of the animal vision and goes directly to the angel Gabriel, who explains the "future" to Daniel in response to his puzzlement over what seemed like an incorrect prophecy of Jeremiah. Daniel has been

> reading the scriptures and reflecting on the seventy years which, according to the word
> of the LORD to the prophet Jeremiah, were to pass while Jerusalem lay in ruins. (9:2)

Here is yet another indication of the date of the Book of Daniel: since the prophetic books were not canonized until about 200 B.C.E., no one would have called Jeremiah "scripture" until after that date; the author of Daniel was writing not very long after Jeremiah and the other prophets were accepted as canonical. From the perspective of the 160's B.C.E., it

HOW 70 YEARS CAN BECOME 490

The author of Daniel ingeniously "predicts" his country's past by re-interpreting Jeremiah's prophecy that "seventy years" would "pass while Jerusalem lay in ruins" (Dan. 9:2).

But hundreds of years after Jeremiah, "calamity" still rules in Jerusalem, Daniel complains (9:12), so the angel Gabriel appears to assure him that Jeremiah really meant not seventy years but "seventy weeks" of years (or 490), a span divided into periods of seven weeks, sixty-two weeks, and one week (49 years, 434 years and 7 years—Dan. 9:24-27).

587 B.C.E. -49 (7 x 7) 538 B.C.E.	Jerusalem destroyed by Babylonian army. "Seven weeks shall pass" (Dan. 9:25), until exiles return from Babylon to rebuild Jerusalem, led by Zerubbabel ("one anointed, a prince"—Dan. 9:25).
	Now Daniel's author must juggle the starting time back to the date of Jeremiah's prophecy:
605 B.C.E. -434 (62 x 7) 171 B.C.E.	"From the time the word went forth that Jerusalem should be restored" (Dan. 9:25), "for sixty-two weeks it shall remain restored" (Dan. 9:25).
	The horror of the last week of years after 171 B. C. E., "havoc on city and sanctuary" (Dan. 9:25), is the point of Daniel's ingenious re-interpretation of Jeremiah.
171 B.C.E.	Israel's High Priest Onias III assassinated: "After the sixty-two weeks, one who is anointed shall be removed" (Dan. 9:26).
171 B.C.E. -3½ (½ week) 167 B.C.E.	"The week half spent," "an invading prince" "shall put a stop to sacrifice and offering" (Dan. 9:26-27): Antiochus IV outlaws Judaism in December, 167 B.C.E. (I Macc. 1:54)
171 B.C.E. -7 164 B.C.E.	For one week," "the horde of an invading prince shall work havoc on city and sanctuary'" (Dan. 9:26-27), until Judas Maccabee re-dedicates the Temple in December, 164 B.C.E. (I Macc. 4:41), 490 years after Jeremiah's re-interpreted prophecy, seventy years becoming seventy weeks of years.

looked as if Jeremiah was wrong when he had declared, about the year 600 B.C.E., that Jerusalem would lie in ruins for a mere seventy years. Four centuries later Jerusalem was suffering "a calamity greater than has ever happened," for the city has a "desolate sanctuary" (Dan. 9:12, 17). What could Jeremiah have meant? The situation of 167 B.C.E., that of the actual author of Daniel, is projected back upon that of the sixth century fictive Daniel, who would have been a contemporary of the historical Jeremiah. Daniel's puzzlement makes perfect sense in the 160s, none at all four hundred years earlier.

In response to Daniel's bewilderment, the angel Gabriel is dispatched to re-interpret Jeremiah, who *really* meant, Daniel learns, not seventy years but "seventy weeks" of years (9:24), a 490-year span divided into periods of weeks of years, seven, sixty-two, and one. Gabriel explains to Daniel that Jeremiah had after all not meant that seventy years would pass between the destruction and rebuilding of Jerusalem, but rather that "from the time that the word went forth that Jerusalem should be restored and rebuilt, seven weeks shall pass till the appearance of one anointed, a prince" (Dan. 9:25)—forty-nine years later, not seventy. Jerusalem was destroyed by the Babylonians in 587 B.C.E., and the rebuilding did indeed commence in 538, forty-nine years later (see Ezra chapter one).

> Of the captives whom King Nebuchadnezzar of Babylon had taken into exile in Babylon, these were the people of the province who returned to Jerusalem and Judah, each to his own town. They were led by Zerubbabel. (Ezra 2:1-2)

This man, a descendant of David, became governor of Judaea and was named by the prophet Haggai as the "chosen" of Yahweh (Haggai 2:23), the "anointed prince," in the words of Gabriel to Daniel.

> Then for sixty-two weeks it shall remain restored, rebuilt with streets and conduits. At the critical time, after the sixty-two weeks, one who is anointed shall be removed with no one to take his part. (Dan. 9:25-26)

Jeremiah had made his "seventy year" prediction in the "fourth year of Jehoiakim son of Josiah, king of Judah," that is, in 605 B.C.E. (Jer. 25:1).

"Sixty-two weeks" of years is 434 years later (62 x 7), or 171 B.C.E., the year that Onias III, High Priest of Israel, was assassinated at the instigation of the usurper Menelaus (II Macc. 4:34) and the removal of this "'anointed" one marked the beginning of the great distress in Jerusalem. After that murder, Daniel is told, "the horde of an invading prince shall work havoc on city and sanctuary" (Dan. 9:26). We know that late in 169 B.C.E. Antiochus IV savagely attacked Jerusalem, killing all the males his soldiers could find and looting the temple (II Macc. 5:11-23; Josephus, *Antiquities 12.5.3*). This was to be followed by the events that evoked the writing of the Book of Daniel:

> Its end shall come with a flood, and to the end there shall be war. Desolations are decreed. He shall make a strong covenant with many for one week, and for half the week he shall make sacrifice and offering cease; and in their place shall be an abomination that desolates. (Dan. 9:26)

Thus the final "week"—171-164 B.C.E.—will see the worst; sacrifice to Yahweh will be replaced by the "abomination," Antiochus' altar to Zeus, on which swine were sacrificed in Jerusalem's temple. The High Priesthood was usurped, first by Jason and then by Menelaus, whose Greek names reveal that they were Antiochus' henchmen in trying to impose Hellenistic culture on Judaea. First Maccabees gives us a most distressing account of these days:

> The king issued an edict throughout his empire: his subjects were all to become one people and abandon their own customs…The king sent agents to Jerusalem and the towns of Judaea with written orders that ways and customs foreign to the country should be introduced…Pagan altars, idols, and sacred precincts were to be established, swine and other unclean beasts to be offered in sacrifice. (I Macc. 1:41-47)

During the final half of that last "week" (167-164 B.C.E.), the altar to Zeus stood in the temple, the "abomination of desolation" (I Macc. 1:54). The author of Daniel was clearly knowledgeable about his own time, and truly ingenious in his re-interpretation of Jeremiah as referring not to the succeeding seventy years after 587 B.C.E. but to the more than four hundred years leading up to Antiochus IV. That he had to do a little juggling among the seven weeks and sixty-two weeks in order to get the dates right only increases one's admiration for his ingenuity. But as is always the case, though the author of Daniel could describe the present, he could not describe the future; for Daniel's next vision predicts the place of death of Antiochus IV, but gets it wrong, the final indication of the Book of Daniel's actual date.

Daniel's supposed visions in chapters seven through ten depict, in progressively more explicit terms as they approach the second century B.C.E., the historical events leading up to the accession of Antiochus IV and his efforts to hellenize Judaea. The eleventh chapter (the next to last of Daniel) gives us a surprisingly detailed account of the immediate predecessors of Antiochus IV, whose rule is called the "time of the end" (Dan. 11:40). The point of the first twenty verses of this chapter is to make perfectly clear that it is indeed Antiochus IV who, as was "predicted," will set up the "abomination of desolation" in Jerusalem (the past of the author of the Book of Daniel is presented in visionary form as the "future" of the fictional Daniel of the sixth century B.C.E.). We learn that the "kingdom of Greece" will be led by a "warrior king" who will arise in opposition to "Persia"; he will rule a "vast kingdom,"

> But as soon as he is established, his kingdom will be shattered and split up north, south, east and west. It will not pass to his descendants. (Dan. 11:3-4)

What do we know about Alexander the Great? He conquered the Persian empire and shortly after died at the age of thirty-two in 323 B.C.E. His realm was divided among his generals, Ptolemy I getting Egypt and Seleucus I getting Syria and Palestine. The classic account of this period, Edwyn R. Bevan's *The House of Seleucus* (1902), informs what follows. Their descendants' bloody history is the point of Daniel 11:5-20, where the "king of the south" (11:5) is Ptolemy and his successors and the "king of the north" (11:6) is Seleucus and his heirs.

> In due course the two will enter into a friendly alliance; to redress the balance the daughter of the king of the south will be given in marriage to the king of the north, but she will

not maintain her influence and their line will not last. She and her escort, her child, and also her lord and master, will be the victims of foul play. (Dan. 11:6)

We know that Antiochus II, grandson of Seleucus I, married Berenice, daughter of Ptolemy II, about 253 B.C.E. in an effort to keep peace between Egypt and Syria. The effort failed, and Berenice and her son by Antiochus were murdered around 246 B.C.E., events followed by the "Third Syrian War" (246-241 B.C.E.). This war was led, on the Egyptian side, by Berenice's brother, Ptolemy III, in events described by the author of Daniel:

Then another shoot from the same stock as hers [Berenice's] will appear in his father's place, will penetrate the defenses of the king of the north and enter his fortress, and will win a decisive victory over his people. (Dan. 11:7)

Seleucus II was defeated by Ptolemy III in this Third Syrian War, just as Daniel said. We know that Seleucus II died in 225 B.C.E. and was succeeded by his son Seleucus III, who was in turn murdered and succeeded by his brother Antiochus III, events briefly summarized in Daniel 11:10:

His [Seleucus II's] sons will press on to assemble a great armed horde. One of them [Antiochus III] will sweep on like an irresistible flood.

We also know that Antiochus III raised an army for the Fourth Syrian War of 221-217 B.C.E., but lost disastrously to Ptolemy IV at Gaza in 217, events described in some detail by the author of Daniel:

The king of the south, his anger roused, will march out to do battle with the king of the north who, in turn, will rouse a great horde, but it will be delivered into the hands of his enemy. When this horde has been captured, the victor will be elated and he will slaughter tens of thousands, yet he will not maintain his advantage. Then the king of the north will once more raise a horde even greater than the last. (Dan. 11:11-13)

It is true that Antiochus III recovered, raised a new army, and finally won the Fifth Syrian War at the Battle of Panium in 200 B.C.E., a victory that gave him control of Palestine, as Daniel 11:16 tells us:

> He will establish himself in the fairest of all lands and it will come wholly into his power. He will resolve to subjugate all the dominions of the south.

Part of his plan was another pretended alliance through marriage, as Antiochus III, under the terms of the peace settlement of 195 B.C.E., gave his daughter Cleopatra I to Ptolemy IV:

> He will come to fair terms with him, and he will give him a young woman in marriage, for the destruction of the kingdom, but she will not persist nor serve his purpose. (Dan. 11:17)

Cleopatra was a better wife than daughter, and when her husband Ptolemy died, she ruled as regent in his stead, becoming more Egyptian than Syrian. Antiochus' plan for Cleopatra a failure, he attempted to enlarge his dominion by invading Thrace, but in so doing he aroused Rome to war against him and was forced back into Syria, events described in Daniel 11:18:

> Then he will turn to the coasts and islands and take many prisoners, but a foreign commander will put an end to his challenge…He will fall back upon his own strongholds; there he will come to disaster and be overthrown and be seen no more.

This is indeed what happened. Antiochus III was killed in Susa in 187 B.C.E. and was succeeded by his son Seleucus IV, who reigned only a few years (187-175 B.C.E.) before being assassinated, as Daniel 11:20 tells us:

> He will be succeeded by one who will send out an officer with a royal escort to extort tribute; after a short time this king too will meet his end, yet neither openly nor in battle.

History tells us that Seleucus IV, according to the terms of the Treaty of Apamea (188 B.C.E.), had to pay a huge indemnity to Rome as a consequence of his father's loss of the Battle of Magnesia two years earlier. Seleucus wanted to pay it with funds confiscated from the temple in Jerusalem (the effort to "extort tribute" mentioned above), but met with such resistance that his effort failed (a legendary account of all this is found in II Maccabees chapter three). Seleucus IV was then assassinated by Heliodorus, and was succeeded by his brother, the "contemptible crea-ture" Antiochus IV (Dan. 11:21), who is the real point of this whole long pretense of prediction. For it is Antiochus IV, King of Syria from 175-164 B.C.E., who will

> vent his fury against the Holy Covenant...Armed forces dispatched by him will dese-crate the sanctuary and the citadel and do away with the regular offering. And there they will set up "the abominable thing that causes desolation." (Dan. 11:30-31)

This is not at all hard to understand. Indeed, the first biblical author to read the Book of Daniel correctly interpreted this passage, applying it to Antiochus IV and his desecration of the temple in 167 B.C.E., as we saw from I Maccabees. Any historically informed reader of the Book of Daniel can work out its meanings, if not blinded by the delusions of apocalypti-cism and its pretense that the distant future was divinely revealed to some ancient seer. Indeed this delusion is what trips up the author of Daniel, who writes that soon after setting up that abomination, the "contemptible creature"

> will depart in a great rage to destroy and exterminate many. He will pitch his royal pavil-ion between the sea and the holy hill, the fairest of all hills; and he will meet his end with no one to help him. (Dan. 11:44-45)

Since the author of Daniel gets the location wrong—Antiochus IV died in Persia in 164 B.C.E. not between the Mediterranean and Jerusalem—we know that the Book of Daniel must have been written *before* this time but *after* Antiochus' desecration of the temple in December, 167 B.C.E. We thus arrive at some time between 166 and 164 as the unmistakable date for the authorship of the Book of Daniel. Its author could clearly describe his own time but, like all of us, he knew lit-tle of the distant past and nothing at all of the future.

Nonetheless, this failed effort to predict the future remained potent and widely read, not least because it provides the first clear teaching in the Bible of the idea of the resurrection of the dead to eternal life. "At that moment," the death of Antiochus IV,

II: Mark's Apocalyptic Mind

> your people will be delivered, every one who is written in the book: many of those who
> sleep in the dust of the earth will wake, some to everlasting life and some to the reproach
> of eternal abhorrence. (Dan. 12:1-2)

The power of this hope, expressed in a vigorous apocalyptic idiom, has kept the Book of Daniel circulating over the centuries, to be re-interpreted again and again as new situations arise.

Late in the first century of our own era there were two remarkable attempts to re-interpret the failed predictions of Daniel as applying not—as had been thought by the author of I Maccabees—to the Seleucid dynasty of Antiochus IV, but to Imperial Rome. One of them was written as an imitation of the Book of Daniel by a Jewish apocalypt pretending to be the sixth-century B.C.E Jewish leader Ezra—we now call it the apocryphal book Fourth Ezra—the other by an anonymous apocalyptic Christian—we now call it the Gospel of Mark.

Fourth Ezra was written during the reign of the Roman emperor Domitian (81-96 C.E.), and like Mark concerns "the problems arising out of the destruction of the temple" in 70 C.E. (*ABD* II,612). It is included in the Apocrypha of the Church of England and of Protestant churches, so the easiest place to find Fourth Ezra is as it is embedded in chapters 3-14 of its later revision, Second Esdras, in the "Apocrypha" section of such translations as the New English Bible, the Revised Standard Version, or their recent revisions.

Since the "fourth beast" of Daniel's vision—the Hellenistic empire of Alexander and his successors, culminating in the "little horn" Antiochus IV—did not prove after all to be the last earthly rulers before the "saints of the Most High" were given "kingly power" (Dan. 7:27), in the eyes of the author of Fourth Ezra the vision needed re-interpreting. He does so in standard apocalyptic form, with a voice from heaven to the fictional "Ezra" who, like Daniel, had been granted a vision of "four beasts," the last one being an eagle, the symbol of the Roman legion. This eagle, Ezra is told, is the "only survivor of the four beasts to which I gave the rule over my world, intending through them to bring my ages to their end" (II Esdras 11:39). The vision is then explained as a re-interpretation of

Daniel's earlier failed prediction. The fourth beast is not the Seleucid empire that succeeded Alexander after all; it is Rome:

Here is the interpretation of your vision. The eagle you saw rising from the sea represents the fourth kingdom in the vision seen by your brother Daniel. But he was not given the interpretation which I am now giving you or have already given you. The days are coming when the earth will be under an empire more terrible than any before. (II Esdras 12:10-13)

There follows a symbolic depiction of the various Roman emperors down to Domitian, who will be, it is predicted, the next to last. "The vision does not know of Domitian's death, which is taken to indicate that *4 Ezra* was written before 96 C.E." (*ABD* II, 613). This figure will rule in the "last years of the empire," and will have only one successor, who will "fall by the sword in the last days" at the hand of the "Messiah whom the Most High has kept back until the end" (II Esdras 12:23, 28, 32). This is not what happened, of course, since the Roman empire continued for centuries after Domitian.

Like all other attempts to predict the future Fourth Ezra failed, but it shows us that the effort to re-interpret the visions of the Book of Daniel as applying "really" to the late first century C.E. is not unique to the New Testament; Mark's effort to do so stands beside a similar and nearly contemporary Jewish work, for apocalypticism was rife throughout the eastern end of the Mediterranean at this time.

The Gospel of Mark was written soon after the year 70 in and for a Christian group that was undergoing intense persecution. It is not surprising that apocalyptic hopes would flourish in such circumstances or that the deliverance promised in the Book of Daniel would be read with joy. As John Dominic Crossan puts it, Mark, writing to a "community that has suffered severely from lethal persecution," performs one of the most typical literary devices of apocalyptic: "He has Jesus foretell as distant future what [Mark] knows full well as immediate past" (1995, 17):

You will be handed over to the courts. You will be flogged in synagogues. You will be summoned to appear before governors and kings on my account. (Mark 13:9)

II: Mark's Apocalyptic Mind

Not only does Mark employ the apocalyptic device of the fictive seer "foretelling" the immediate past of the author, he uses the very words of the Book of Daniel in its Septuagint Greek version as the basis for Jesus' "prediction" of the destruction of Jerusalem in 70 C.E. Mark is the first Christian writer to do so, the first to perceive that Daniel was "really" about the Jewish war with Rome rather than the Maccabean war with Syria, and the first to see the destruction of Jerusalem in 70 as the prelude to what Daniel called the coming of the son of man on the clouds of heaven to establish the kingdom of God.

The thirteenth chapter of Mark is the center of this effort; here Jesus is represented as predicting that "Not one stone will be left upon another," that Jerusalem's temple would be razed to the ground (Mark 13:2), as did indeed happen at the order of Titus in September, 70 (Josephus, 361). It may well be that Mark had heard that one "Jesus" had foretold the destruction of Jerusalem, and he took this figure to be Jesus of Nazareth. According to Josephus, Jesus the son of Ananias had gone about Jerusalem for "seven years and five months," starting about the year 62, crying "woe to the City, the people and the Sanctuary." When arrested by the Procurator Albinus to be scourged and interrogated, "he made no reply whatever to the questions but endlessly repeated his lament over the city" (Josephus, 350). This sounds strangely like events in the Gospel of Mark: prediction of the city's woe, arrest by the Procurator Pontius Pilate, scourging, silence under questioning. Believing that Jesus had predicted the temple's destruction, knowing it had been destroyed, Mark set about understanding this in the light of his reading of the Book of Daniel.

Using the Greek Septuagint version of the apocalyptic discourses in Daniel as his model, Mark presented in his thirteenth chapter an apocalyptic discourse of Jesus in which Jesus' future (that is, Mark's present and near past) is regarded as foreordained and predetermined. Just as Daniel revealed to Nebuchadnezzar "what must take place [*dei genesthai*] in the last days" (Dan. 2:28 LXX), so Jesus reveals to his disciples what "must take place [*dei genesthai*] before the end" (Mark 13:7). When Antiochus IV set up an altar to Zeus in Jerusalem's temple in 167 B.C.E., I Maccabees calls it the "abomination of desolation" (1:54). The Greek version of Daniel calls it the same, "the abomination of desolation [*to bdelygma erēmōseōs*]," declaring that its establishment presages the "time of the end," a time of "tribulation as has not been [*thlipsis hoia ou gegonen*]" (Dan. 12:1, 11 LXX).

Likewise for Mark, the setting up of the "abomination of desolation [*bdelygma tēs erēmōseōs*]" will be a time of "tribulation as has not been [*thlipsis hoia ou gegonen*]" (Mark 13:19). We know from Josephus that in August of the year 70, "the Romans brought their standards into the Temple area, and erecting them opposite the East Gate sacrificed to them there, and with thunderous acclamations hailed Titus as *Imperator*" (351). Mark is directly dependent upon the vocabulary of Septuagint Daniel in his effort to understand the events of 70. Mark's thirteenth chapter gives us not an actual speech of the historical Jesus, whose language was Aramaic, but a statement from Mark himself in the literary form of apocalyptic discourse about his own time. In this chapter, Mark is as fully apocalyptic as the Book of Daniel, and just as wrong in his predictions.

Like the author of Daniel, Mark was convinced that the presence of the "abomination of desolation" meant that "the end is near" (Mark 13:14,29). In practical terms, however, what the Roman destruction of Jerusalem meant for the future of Christianity was the end of the Jewish Christianity of Palestine, the end of the Jerusalem-centered church that had been led by James the brother of Jesus, and the opportunity for the triumph of the Gentile Christian mission Paul had started in the forties. Mark, a Gentile Christian, believed in that mission and has Jesus predict it in chapter thirteen: "before the end the gospel must be proclaimed to all nations" (13:10). Remember that for Mark this word "nations" (*ethne*) really meant "Gentiles," not "countries." The Gentile Christian Mission succeeded (that is, Christianity became a non-Jewish religion) as a direct consequence of the depopulation of Judaea after 70. The "new age" Mark has Jesus predict turns out to be a new religion, the Christianity we know today.

Just as the author of Daniel was wrong in his apocalyptic expectation that Antiochus' establishing the altar to Zeus in the temple meant that within three and a half years his "people will be delivered" (Dan. 12:1,12), Mark was equally wrong in his hope that Roman sacrifices to the eagle standard in the temple in August, 70, meant that "the end is near, at the very door" (Mark 13:30). Apocalyptic predictions of "the end of this age" (Dan. 2:28) are necessarily self-disconfirming, and always have to be re-interpreted by the next generation that was not supposed to appear. As we shall see, this was the case with the gospels of Matthew, Luke, and John, all three written in the next generation in part as responses to Mark. They may be described as unsuccessful efforts to outgrow Mark's failed eschatology.

❧ III ❧

THE MIND OF MATTHEW

MATTHEW'S IS ONE MIND of the ancient world we can actually see at work. We can picture Matthew at his writing table, composing his gospel, choosing one word rather than another, because we possess the book he had open in front of him as he wrote: the Gospel of Mark, his major source. According to B. H. Streeter, "Matthew is a fresh edition of Mark, revised, rearranged, and enriched with new material" (1951, 159). Of the 666 verses in Mark, some 600 appear in Matthew, most of them rewritten but containing, in hundreds of instances, the same words in the same order. That there is a literary relationship between the Gospels of Mark and Matthew has been recognized since at least the time of St. Augustine of Hippo in the fifth century, but his notion—that Mark is a condensed version of Matthew (as opposed to Matthew's being an expanded Mark)—has been abandoned by all responsible scholars except the fundamentalists who cling to the wishful notion that the First Gospel comes from the hand of the Apostle Matthew himself. Robert Gundry concludes that since it "is supposed that no apostle [like Matthew] would have used the work of a non-apostle [like Mark]" (1982, 49), these wishful thinkers reject the Two-Source Theory and point to Papias, as reported by Eusebius:

> Matthew composed the Logia (*ta logia*) in the Hebrew tongue and everyone interpreted them as he was able. (Eusebius iii,39,16)

But the Gospel of Matthew is written in Greek; it uses Greek sources (Mark, Q, and the Septuagint Bible) and could not have been written in Hebrew (or Aramaic either). Nor is Matthew just "Logia" (sayings). Whatever Papias means, it is not the Gospel of Matthew.

LEVELS OF REMOVE FROM THE HISTORICAL JESUS:

1. Personal associates of Jesus

2. Christian oral traditions about Jesus

3. Written documents based on oral traditions

4. Mark

5. Matthew.

If Mark stands at the fourth remove from the historical Jesus, Matthew's use of Mark puts him at the fifth.

Matthew uses Mark; if Mark stands at the fourth remove from Jesus, then Matthew stands at the fifth: 1. personal associates of Jesus; 2. Christian oral tradition about Jesus; 3. written documents about Jesus using oral traditions; 4. Mark; 5. Matthew. At each remove, connection to the historical Jesus lessens. This is not to imply that Mark is thus historically "more accurate" than Matthew, for theological fiction is already fully developed at the second remove and continues at each succeeding stage, as we shall see happening in Matthew's use of Mark's account of Jesus' baptism.

Mark's baptism story provided several major challenges to Matthew's mind and art. It was Matthew's source for his baptism account, but some of its theological implications troubled Matthew so much that one wonders why he even used it. Matthew must have felt *compelled* to tell about John the Baptist; since Jesus' message (Matt. 4:17) exactly repeated John's, word for word (Matt. 3:2), and coming after John's was thus imitative and not original, Matthew must have felt a strong need to differentiate between the two figures and give them their proper Christian ranking. So he demotes John from Jesus' mentor to his advance-man: John was Elijah-come-back before the apocalyptic "terrible day" (in fulfillment of Malachi 4:5), to "Prepare a way for the Lord" (in fulfillment of Isa. 40:3).

III: The Mind of Matthew

Matthew borrows this interpretation from Mark, though correcting Mark's insufficiently critical use of it as we saw earlier (Mark thought he was quoting Isaiah rather than from a garbled version of Malachi); now Matthew sees another failing in Mark's baptism story: its theological implications were intolerable. Mark wrote that John "came proclaiming a baptism in token of repentance for sins; and they flocked to him from the whole Judaean country-side and the city of Jerusalem, and were baptized by him in the River Jordan, confessing their sins." Therefore "Jesus came from Nazareth in Galilee and was baptized in the Jordan by John" (Mark 1:4-5,9). Mark seems not to mind his implication that Jesus was just another sinner seeking forgiveness. Matthew minded a great deal and took steps to reverse that implication, granting to John the insight (found in no other gospel) that Jesus did not *need* baptism: "Do you come to me?...I need rather to be baptized by you" (Matt. 3:14). This passage allows us our first major insight into the mind of Matthew: that for him theological considerations outweigh his own self-critical powers; he will forget himself in his anxiety to make a theological point. For here Matthew suddenly imputes superhuman knowledge to John the Baptist, making him recognize at once Jesus' identity and sinlessness, and forgetting that in chapter eleven of his gospel he has reduced John once again to a normal human perplexity about Jesus: "John, who was in prison, heard what Christ was doing, and sent his own disciples to him with this message: 'Are you the one who is to come, or are we to expect some other?'" (Matt. 11:2-3).

Matthew is exceptionally clear-sighted and critical about his source, Mark, but insufficiently critical of his own narrative inventiveness as theologian; his critical powers are weaker toward himself than toward others—an unsurprising fact since this is true of us all.

Jesus' baptism by one calling sinners to repentance was equally troubling to Luke and John. Luke dealt with the problem by describing Jesus' baptism only after the arrest of John, calling it a "general" baptism, performed apparently by some other unnamed person for whom repentance was not the issue (Luke 3:21). The Gospel of John goes even farther, neglecting to state that Jesus was baptized at all! John the Baptist is present only to point out Jesus as the "Lamb of God" (John 1:29).

Matthew's next problem with Mark's baptism story concerns the voice from heaven; in Mark it looks like a private revelation to Jesus of information he did not have before: "At the moment when he came up out of the water, he saw the heavens torn open and the spirit, like a dove, descending upon him. And a voice spoke from heaven: 'Thou art my Son, my Beloved; on thee my favor rests'" (Mark 1:10-11).

Matthew, however, has just given two chapters to an account of the Virgin Birth and an angel's assurance to Joseph that Mary has conceived by the Holy Spirit; surely Matthew's Jesus would have learned from his parents this wonderful fact and would need no voice from heaven to tell him whose son he really is. Matthew's first two chapters have rendered Mark's account of the voice from heaven quite redundant. Mark had written under a double compulsion: to present the anointing of Jesus as Son and Messiah while abiding by the theme of the Messianic Secret—a theory that *required* the voice to be a private revelation only to Jesus. Thus in Mark Jesus alone sees the vision: "he saw the heavens torn open and the Spirit, like a dove, descending." But Mark's source for the voice from heaven, not being bound by Mark's theme of the Messianic Secret, does not present the voice as a private revelation, and Mark fails to correct that impression: the voice "spoke from heaven," presumably for anyone to hear. We know where Mark's source got the words "Thou art my son," for they come directly from the Septuagint Greek of Ps. 2:7: "The Lord said unto me, thou art my son, today I have begotten thee," words that follow the statement, "I have been made king by him" (Ps. 2:6 LXX).

Matthew almost certainly knew about, and would have read as oracular, this passage in the second Psalm, but what he didn't realize was that his problem with the voice from heaven in Mark's baptism scene stems from the fact that placing "Thou art my Son" *at the baptism* is Mark's own fiction. Years before Mark's Gospel, "Thou art my Son" had appeared in Christian tradition as a *resurrection* statement; and Mark in fact possessed two stories in which a voice from heaven identified Jesus as the

Son of God. Both of them were originally resurrection-appearance stories, but since Mark as we know chose not to present any resurrection appearances of Jesus (for in his view Jesus' next appearance would be at the Second Coming, just two or three years, Mark thought, in his future), he back-dated the two stories as events in the earthly career of Jesus: we know them now as the Baptism and the Transfiguration.

The voice from heaven in Mark's baptism scene began in Christian tradition as a resurrection statement. Already in the fifties of the first century Ps. 2:7 was read by Christians as an oracle of Jesus' resurrection. Paul wrote to the Romans that Jesus was "declared Son of God by a mighty act in that he rose from the dead" (Romans 1:4), while in Acts, Luke makes explicit the biblical reference Paul had in mind, having Paul declare in Pisidian Antioch "the good news that God, who made the promise to the fathers, has fulfilled it for the children by raising Jesus from the dead, as indeed it stands written, in the second Psalm: "You are my son; this day I have begotten you" (Acts 13:32-33). The other resurrection narrative that Mark back-dated as a voice from heaven identifying the Earthly Jesus as Son of God appears now as the Transfiguration, where a voice from heaven declares, "This is my Son, my Beloved; listen to him" (Mark 9:7). This passage gives us the clue to Matthew's solution of his problem with Mark's baptism scene.

Matthew was uncomfortable with Mark's account of the voice from heaven at the baptism; a revelation to Jesus that he was Son of God seemed quite superfluous after two chapters making clear that Jesus is Son of God because God made his mother pregnant. But how can Matthew change his source? Having, naturally, already read Mark all the way through, he would have remembered the Transfiguration; opening Mark to that scene, he found the words he needed: "This is my Son, my Beloved" (Mark 9:7). Here is the source of the words from heaven in Matthew's version of the baptism story; Matthew is not encumbered by Mark's theory of the Messianic Secret, so he can readily make the dove and the voice from heaven clear to all present, resolving both the ambiguity in Mark's account and the clash with Matthew's own first two chapters: "After baptism Jesus came up out of the water at once; and at that moment heaven opened; he saw the Spirit of God descending like a dove to alight upon him; and a voice from heaven was heard saying, 'This is my Son, my Beloved, on whom my favor rests'" (Matt. 3:16-17).

It is not Jesus who needs telling who he is, but others. We can even prove that Matthew used the voice from heaven in Mark's Transfiguration as the source for the voice from heaven in his own baptism account. When Matthew came to write his own story of the Transfiguration (an episode in Mark he could not understand anyway, not knowing it was a back-dated resurrection appearance, so he downgraded it from literal experience to a "vision"—Matt. 17:9), he changed Mark's "This is my Son, my Beloved; listen to him" to match his own wording of the voice at the baptism: "This is my Son, my Beloved, on whom my favor rests; listen to him" (Matt. 17:5). So in Matthew the baptism story is changed on the basis of Mark's Transfiguration scene, and then Matthew bases his version of the Transfiguration in turn on his changed version of the baptism. Matthew is at least consistent.

Matthew is, in other words, quite critical in his use of Mark, correcting Mark not only in theology but in his use of the Bible as well. We can readily imagine Matthew at his writing table with both Mark and a copy of the Greek Septuagint Bible open in front of him, first reading Mark and then checking Mark's use of Scripture before writing his own version of Mark's story. For in his reading of Mark he observed that Mark generally quotes not from the Bible but from some source originating in oral tradition that has been based on the Bible, and does not appear to have checked his source's accuracy. Our first example of this stands in Matthew's changing of Mark's citation of "Isaiah" in his introduction of John the Baptist. Mark did not appear to be aware, as I showed earlier, that half his supposed citation of Isaiah is in fact a garbled mixture of Malachi 3:1 and Exodus 23:20. But Matthew read Mark carefully, grasped the error, checked Septuagint Isaiah to make sure, and then corrected Mark's mistake by quoting only the words from Isaiah 40:3. Strangely, however, he kept Mark's paraphrase of the last part of the Isaiah passage, an action that is quite revealing of

III: The Mind of Matthew

Matthew's mind:

> It is of him that the prophet Isaiah spoke when he said, "A voice crying aloud in the wilderness, 'Prepare a way for the Lord; clear a straight path for him.'" (Matt. 3:3)

Septuagint Isaiah has instead "Prepare the way of the Lord, make straight the paths of our God" (40:3); both Mark and Matthew were comfortable with calling Jesus "Lord," but neither felt at ease calling him "God." So even though Matthew seems to have checked Mark's citation and corrected it by dropping the passages not from Isaiah, he did not correct the end of the citation, leaving it in Mark's form; although it was scripturally inaccurate, it was more theologically correct than precise use of Isaiah would allow.

Valid understanding of Jesus through accurate citation of the Bible is the key to grasping another example of Matthew's correction of Mark, in the scene where Jesus tells why he speaks in parables. Mark gives us a shockingly strange account of the scene, showing Jesus citing Scripture to explain that he speaks in parables so that most people will *not* be able to understand his teachings:

> [T]he Twelve and others who were round him questioned him about the parables. He replied, "To you the secret of the kingdom of God has been given; but to those who are outside everything comes by way of parables, so that (as Scripture says) they may look and look, but see nothing; they may hear and hear, but understand nothing; otherwise they might turn to God and be forgiven." (Mark 4:10-12)

It is not hard to imagine Matthew reading this and scratching his head in wonderment. Being deeply familiar with the Bible, he knew about parables and their clear and obvious teachings, knew about the parable of the trees (Judges 9) and the parables of Nathan and the wise woman of Tekoah (II Sam. 12 and 14). Parables *elucidate*, they don't obfuscate. Matthew knew he had to correct Mark's misunderstanding; reading again, he saw the reference to Scripture, recognized a paraphrase of Isaiah, looked up the passage (Isa. 6:9-10), and quoted it exactly from the Septuagint in place of Mark's paraphrase: the quotation readily provides the basis for Matthew's correction of Mark's misunderstanding of parables:

> The disciples went up to him and asked, "Why do you speak to them in parables?" He replied, "It has been granted to you to know the secrets of the kingdom of Heaven; but to those others it has not been granted…That is why I speak to them in parables; for they look without seeing, and listen without hearing or understanding. There is a prophecy of Isaiah which is being fulfilled for them: 'You may hear and hear, but you will never understand; you may look and look, but you will never see. For this people's mind has become gross; their ears are dulled, and their eyes are closed. Otherwise their eyes might see, their ears hear, and their mind understand, and then they might turn again, and I would heal them.'" (Matt. 13:10-15)

Matthew changes Mark's notion that Jesus spoke in parables "so that" people might "hear but understand nothing" to a much more sensible view: parables were meant to *help* people understand the ideas of Jesus.

Matthew's correction of Mark's biblical ignorance extends even to what may appear to be minor matters of citation. If Mark, for example, presents Jesus citing Scripture wrongly, Matthew will silently correct the error; when the Pharisees complain that Jesus' disciples were plucking grain on the Sabbath, Mark has Jesus argue, "Have you not read what David did when he and his men were hungry and had nothing to eat? He went into the House of God, in the time of Abiathar the High Priest, and ate the sacred bread" (Mark 2:25-26).

Actually, the High Priest at the time was Ahimelech, Abiathar's father (II Sam. 21:1-6). Matthew assumes that Jesus would certainly know Scripture better than this, and changes Mark by dropping the incorrect name: "Have you not read what David did when he and his men were hungry? He went into the House of God and ate the sacred bread" (Matt. 12:3-4). And when, in the story of the rich young ruler, Mark has Jesus misquote the Ten Commandments, Matthew again silently corrects the error, while also changing Mark's "incorrect" theology about Jesus' goodness:

> a stranger ran up, and, kneeling before him, asked, "Good Master, what must I do to win eternal life?" Jesus said to him, "Why do you call me good? No one is good except God alone. You know the commandments: 'Do not murder; do not commit adultery; do not steal; do

III: The Mind of Matthew

not give false evidence; do not defraud; honor your father and mother.'" (Mark 10:17-19)

Mark has Jesus invent a new commandment, "do not defraud," and asserts that Jesus denied he is "good"—both unacceptable to Matthew, so he changes Mark:

> a man came up and asked him, "Master, what good must I do to gain eternal life?" "Good," said Jesus, "why do you ask me about that? One alone is good. But if you wish to enter into life, keep the commandments." "Which commandments?" he asked. Jesus answered, "Do not murder; do not commit adultery; do not steal; do not give false evidence; honor your father and mother." (Matt. 19:16-19)

Matthew drops "do not defraud," changes "Good Master, what must I do?" to "Master, what good must I do?" and changes "Why do you call me good?" to "Good? Why do you ask me about that?" These corrections may seem trivial, but clearly they have more to do with theological understanding of Jesus than with accurate reporting of events. For Matthew, like all of the gospel writers, was much less interested in reporting events than in presenting theology; Matthew was not averse to creating theological fiction in order to tell his truth about Jesus. We find a clear example of this when Matthew deals with Mark's report that, on Jesus' visit to his hometown of Nazareth, the villagers fail to appreciate him, knowing all too well his family and background—a reception that unnerves Jesus and limits his healing powers:

> "Is not this the carpenter, the son of Mary, the brother of James and Joseph and Judas and Simon? And are not his sisters here with us?" So they fell foul of him. Jesus said to them, "A prophet will always be held in honor except in his home town, and among his kinsmen and family." He could work no miracle there, except that he put his hands on a few sick people and healed them; and he was taken aback by their want of faith. (Mark 6:3-6)

In his treatment of Mark's episode, Matthew reveals himself as something of a snob (making Jesus not the carpenter but the carpenter's son), and in his eagerness not to admit any limitations to Jesus' power, turns him into a spiteful person:

> "Is he not the carpenter's son? Is not his mother called Mary, his brothers James, Joseph,

Who Wrote The Gospels?

Simon and Judas? And are not all his sisters here with us? Where then has he got all this from?" So they fell foul of him , and this led him to say, "A prophet will always be held in honor, except in his home town, and in his own family." And he did not work many miracles there, such was their want of faith. (Matt. 13:55-58)

Mark's Jesus is rather touchingly "taken aback" by his reception in Nazareth, losing some of his miraculous powers; he seems more human and likeable. Matthew's, on the other hand, deliberately refuses—in retaliation for his home town's inability to take him seriously—to alleviate the suffering of some of his own neighbors. Matthew's Jesus may be more in control of his own powers, but he is a much less likeable figure.

Mark has yet another story showing that Jesus' own family does not hold him in honor, one that Matthew again finds troubling. In Mark's third chapter Jesus' family, on learning that he was going about calling himself the Son of Man and forgiving people their sins, become convinced that he has taken leave of his senses: "When his family heard of this, they set out to take charge of him. 'He is out of his mind,' they said" (Mark 3:21). A few verses later, we learn the identity of these family members: "his mother and his brothers arrived, and remaining outside, sent in a message asking him to come out to them" (Mark 12:46). Matthew repeats part of this story, telling about Jesus' family arriving while he is teaching and "wanting to speak to him" (Matt. 3:31), but fails entirely to describe their motivation for doing so, not wanting to repeat Mark's explanation (Jesus' presumed insanity) for their seeking him out. Matthew could not allow *his* Mary such a thought about her son; surely she would have known about what the angel had told Joseph. Mark's Mary clearly knows none of this, and is only worried about a son who is acting strangely. In other words, we don't have "Mary," we have Mark's Mary and Matthew's Mary, two different fictional characters. One can say the same about Mark's and Matthew's Jesus.

Matthew's Jesus, unlike Mark's, has no limits to his powers, as Matthew's treatment of Mark's story of the cursing of the fig tree shows: "He felt hungry, and, noticing in the distance a fig-tree in leaf, he went to see if he could find anything on it. But when he came there he found nothing but leaves; for it was not the season for figs. He said to the tree, 'May no one ever again eat fruit from you!' (Mark 11:13-14). Mark gives us a rather endearingly human Jesus, hungry and exasperated, one who has forgotten that it is not fig-season and who makes a wasted trip to a fruitless tree. And in Mark it is not until the next day that the disciples see the withered tree, dead in response to Jesus' anger. Matthew treats the story quite differently: "He felt hungry; and seeing a fig-tree at the roadside he went up to it, but found nothing on it but leaves. He said to the tree, 'You shall never bear fruit any more!'; and the tree withered away at once" (Matt. 21:19).

Matthew's Jesus, so filled with supernatural powers, cannot be allowed to be ignorant of the time of year, so Matthew drops Mark's statement that it was "not the season for figs"; and Matthew cannot allow Jesus to walk into "the distance," not knowing all the while whether there will be figs, so he places the tree at the "roadside." Since Matthew has dropped Mark's statement that "it was not the season for figs," Matthew puts the fault on the tree for not having fruit, the fig-tree is barren; thus Jesus does not have to appear so humanly exasperated, so limited and like ourselves. And of course in Matthew the tree withers away "at once," with no day-long delay as in Mark.

Again it is clear that Matthew sees his task as presenting correct theological interpretation of Jesus, not describing "what happened"; he had already in Mark an account of the supposed event, but that account did not present Jesus in the light Matthew wanted. "Religious fiction" is a good term for what Matthew is doing here, and this episode gives us marvelous insight into his mind, a mind holding that "truth" about Jesus means seeing him reverently as one who possesses not human limitations but divine power.

And the disciples, too, must be presented as having this same kind of reverence toward Jesus. Matthew's treatment of Mark's account of the stilling of the storm shows this clearly. In Mark, the frightened disciples speak rudely to Jesus: "Master, we are sinking! Do you not care?" (Mark 4:38).

Wanting to present the disciples in a different light, Matthew changes their outburst to a prayer of faith: "Save us, Lord; we are sinking!" (Matt. 8:35). Throughout his gospel, Matthew consistently changes the picture of the disciples he found in Mark. In the earlier gospel, just as the citizens of Nazareth fail to understand Jesus, so do his own followers; they never really grasp the point even of the Crucifixion. In chapter nine of Mark, Jesus tells his disciples, for the second time, that soon he must be killed and then three days later rise again: "But they did not understand what he said, and were afraid to ask" (Mark 9:32). Matthew repeats the second Passion Prediction point for point, but drastically changes the disciples' reaction: "they were filled with grief" (Matt. 17:23).

Mark deliberately presents the disciples as limited, even obtuse, never quite able to understand the teachings or mission of their Master; not only do they fail to grasp the point of the Cross, they don't understand the idea of resurrection either. After the Transfiguration, Mark, in keeping with his theme of the Messianic Secret, has Jesus instruct his disciples "not to tell anyone what they had seen until the Son of Man had risen from the dead. They seized upon these words, and discussed among themselves what this 'rising from the dead' could mean" (Mark 9:9-10).

Matthew, a Jewish Christian who knew that resurrection of the dead was a central teaching in the Book of Daniel and an article of faith among Pharisees, couldn't imagine how Jesus' Jewish disciples would not know about resurrection, and so drops Mark's entire verse (9:10) from his own retelling of Mark's story. In Mark, Jesus tries yet a third time to explain to his uncomprehending disciples the necessity of his Passion and Resurrection, and they fail again to understand; indeed two of those disciples, James and John, still failing to grasp the point of the Passion after this third explanation, ask instead for personal aggrandizement:

> James and John, the sons of Zebedee, approached him and said, "Master, we should like you to do us a favor." "What is it you want me to do?" he asked. They answered, "Grant us the right to sit in state with you, one at your right and the other at your left." Jesus said to them, "You [plural] do not understand what you [plural] are asking." (Mark 10:35-38)

III: The Mind of Matthew

Matthew, not wanting to present James and John as such selfish and grasping persons, so insensitive to their Master's approaching Passion, puts this request on the lips of their mother, who lovingly seeks the honor for them:

> The mother of Zebedee's sons then came before him, with her sons. She bowed low and begged a favor. "What is it you wish?" asked Jesus. "I want you," she said, "to give orders that in your kingdom my two sons here may sit next to you, one at your right, and the other at your left." Jesus answered, "You [plural] do not understand what you [plural] are asking." (Matt. 20:20-22)

In his haste to protect the reputations of James and John, Matthew has left Jesus' answer to her in the plural as he copies it from Mark, forgetting that Jesus is supposedly answering the request of one person. Or, alternatively, Matthew is attributing supernatural insight to Jesus, who has grasped that James and John have put their mother forward to speak for them. In this case, Matthew has forgotten that though *he* knows (from Mark) that the outrageous request really comes from James and John, his readers, who do not have Mark open in front of them as he does, would not know this; so his imputation of supernatural insight to Jesus is pointless. In either case, Matthew is touchingly like ourselves in his forgetfulness. The most striking example of Matthew's forgetfulness in his haste to make a theological point stands in his version of Jesus' "sign of Jonah" saying. Mark has Jesus reject the whole concept of signs:

> to test him they asked for a sign from heaven. He sighed deeply to himself and said, "Why does this generation ask for a sign? I tell you this: no sign shall be given to this generation." (Mark 8:11-12)

In his version of this scene, Matthew adds a phrase from source Q:

> To test him they asked him to show them a sign from heaven. His answer was, "It is a wicked generation that asks for a sign; and the only sign that will be given it is the sign of Jonah." (Matt. 16:1-4)

Here, Matthew does not say what that sign is because has already done so, four chapters earlier:

The only sign that will be given it is the sign of the prophet Jonah. Jonah was in the sea-monster's belly for three days and three nights, and in the same way the Son of Man will be three days and three nights in the bowels of the earth. (Matt. 12:39-40)

In his haste to show that the career of Jesus is foreshadowed in the Scriptures, Matthew has forgotten that in his own story, Jesus is buried just before sundown on Friday and the tomb is found empty at daybreak on Sunday—one day and two nights later. We know that the mathematical weakness here is Matthew's own, that he has himself invented this explanation of the "sign of Jonah," because Luke also got the "sign of Jonah" from Q and invented another rather more sensible interpretation of its meaning: "the only sign that will be given it is the sign of Jonah. For just as Jonah was a sign to the Ninevites, so will the Son of Man be to this generation...for they repented at the preaching of Jonah; and what is here is greater than Jonah" (Luke 11:29-30, 32).

Matthew's determination to show that the career of Jesus, including minor details, was predicted in the Scriptures—even if presenting such fulfillment results in absurdity—shows best in his treatment of Mark's account of the Triumphal Entry:

He sent two of his disciples with these instructions: "Go to the village opposite, and, just as you enter, you will find tethered there a colt which no one has yet ridden. Untie it and bring it here.... So they brought the colt to Jesus and spread their cloaks on it, and he mounted. (Mark 11:2, 7)

Matthew's revision of this account shows how seriously he treats the "accurate" fulfillment of what he takes to be prediction of Jesus' career:

Jesus sent two disciples with these instructions: "Go to the village opposite, where you will at once find a donkey tethered with her foal beside her; untie them and bring them to me." ...This was to fulfill the prophecy which says, "Tell the daughter of Zion, 'Here is your king, who comes to you in gentleness, riding on an ass, riding on the foal of a beast of burden.'" The disciples went and did as Jesus had directed, and brought the donkey and her foal; they laid their cloaks on them and Jesus mounted them. (Matt. 21:1-2, 4-7)

Here the New English Bible masks the real meaning of Matthew's

III: The Mind of Matthew

Greek, leaving out that last word "them" (*auton*) in order to eliminate the strangeness of this scene. For Matthew had grasped Mark's apparent ignorance that his source for the account of the Triumphal Entry was based on an oracular reading of Zechariah 9:9, so Matthew quotes that passage to make the "fulfillment" explicit—indeed absurdly so. Zechariah had written poetically, in the Hebrew literary form known as "parallelism," a rhetorical pattern in which a statement is first made and then its idea repeated in different words. Matthew reads the parallelism literally, as if two animals are involved, and doubles Mark's one colt into a colt plus its mother, giving us the absurdity of Jesus mounting them both at once, like a trick rodeo-rider.

The final revision of Mark in the direction of theological accuracy that I wish to discuss stands in Matthew's apocalyptic twenty-fourth chapter, his version of Mark's thirteenth. Writing perhaps a generation after Mark, Matthew saw how wrong Mark had been in his expectation that the Son of Man would come again three and a half years after 70 C.E. Mark's gospel badly needed revising in this regard, and Matthew was the first to do so.

Mark had depicted Jesus correctly foretelling the destruction of Jerusalem and its temple two days before his arrest in the spring of the year 30 (on the date see Meier 402). Jesus' disciples, on being told that "not one stone will be left upon another" (Mark 13:2), naturally want to know "when will this happen?" (Mark 13:4). Mark's Jesus proceeds to make it clear, in the fifth through the twenty-third verses of this thirteenth chapter, that the period from his crucifixion to the destruction of the temple would be much longer than the period between the destruction of the temple and the coming of the Son of Man on the clouds. Mark first describes an extended period after Jesus' departure (forty years, as it turned out), in which there would be battles "near at hand" and "far away," "earthquakes," "famines," proclamation of the Gospel "to all nations," and intense persecution of Christians: "All will hate you for your allegiance to me; but the man who holds out to the end will be saved."

But then Jesus' followers would "see 'the abomination of desolation' usurping a place which is not his," an event that "will bring distress such as never has been until now. If the Lord had not cut short that time of troubles, no living thing could survive. However, for the sake of his own, whom he has chosen, he has cut short the time." (Mark 13:14, 19, 20)

This brings us up to Mark's own time, soon after the terrible events of the year 70; all the signs had come to pass save one. Then Mark looks forward to his own near-term future: "But in those days, after that distress, the sun will be darkened, the moon will not give her light; the stars will come falling from the sky, the celestial powers will be shaken. Then they will see the Son of Man coming in the clouds" (Mark 13:24-26). For Mark, the "great distress" had been cut short, Jerusalem had fallen; there remained only the heavenly portents: "When you see all this happening, you may know that the end is near, at the very door. I tell you this: the present generation will live to see it all" (Mark 13:29-30)—will live, that is, to see both the destruction of Jerusalem and the coming on the clouds of the Son of Man.

Mark had been wrong, and needed revising; Matthew begins this process right at the beginning of his version of Mark chapter thirteen. As in Mark, Matthew's Jesus declares that "not one stone will be left upon another." But when the disciples, seeking clarification, ask, "When will this happen?", Matthew adds a sentence not in Mark: "And what will be the signal for your coming and the end of the world?" (Matt. 24:3) In other words, the destruction of Jerusalem will not be, for Matthew as it had been for Mark, the "signal" for Jesus' Second Coming; the better part of a generation had passed since the distress of 70 and the world continued. Matthew wants to make clear that the period of time between Jerusalem's destruction and the Second Coming will be about the same length as the period of time between Jesus' death and the destruction of Jerusalem, perhaps forty years. Mark had written just after the "time of trouble" of the Jewish War had ended: "he has cut short the time" (Mark 13:20). But from his perspective, perhaps around 90 C.E., Matthew has grasped that the time of trouble must extend for some period *after* the destruction of Jerusalem; so he changes the wording in his revision of Mark 13:20:

It will be a time of great distress; there never has been such a time from the beginning of the world until now, and will never be again. If that time of troubles were not cut short, no living thing could survive; but for the sake of God's chosen it will be cut short. (Matt. 24:21-22)

For Matthew, the time of troubles is *now*, perhaps twenty years after 70 C.E., and it *will* mercifully be cut short soon, whereas for Mark, the time of distress "*has*" been cut short at the year 70. Mark had been wrong, and his false expectations had troubled many when they failed, so Matthew adds two sentences after his revision of Mark 13:9, as if Jesus had warned us in advance about Mark: "Many will fall from their faith; they will betray one another and hate one another. Many false prophets will arise, and will mislead many" (Matt. 24:10-11).

These verses are not in Mark, and seem addressed directly to the effects of Mark's miscalculation. Whereas for Mark, the distress was over and the heavenly portents were coming directly, for Matthew, the distress had continued for twenty-odd years, and will end soon. In place of Mark's "in those days, after that distress, the sun will be darkened" (Mark 13:24), Matthew writes "As soon as the distress of those days has passed, the sun will be darkened" (Matt. 24:29). Then Matthew adds another sentence to his revision of Mark, and gives himself away. Whereas Mark had been supposedly quoting from a speech of Jesus in Aramaic—even though Mark was dependent upon the Greek of the Septuagint for the meanings of his thirteenth chapter—Matthew cannot keep himself from making a Greek pun: "All the peoples of the earth will make lamentation [*kopsontai*], and they will see [*opsontai*] the Son of Man coming on the clouds of heaven" (Matt. 24:30). Matthew adds his own fictional artistic touch to Mark's great fictional apocalyptic discourse, revealing his own hand and mind, not that of Jesus.

Finally, to clinch his point that there would be a much longer period between Jerusalem's destruction and the Second Coming than Mark had imagined, Matthew adds, in the next chapter, a series of parables about the long delay of that Coming. First, we learn about the "bad servant," who "says to himself, 'The master is a long time coming'" and neglects his duties (Matt. 25:48); then about the foolish virgins, who took no oil for their lamps, and "As the bridegroom was late in coming," they had no light for him (Matt. 25:5). Again, Matthew has Jesus tell a parable about " a man going abroad" who left money for his servants to invest. "A long time afterward, their master returned" to settle accounts (Matt. 25:14,19). All three of these parables concern what has come to be called the theme of the "delay of the *Parousia*," the fact that contrary to Mark's expectation, the Master was indeed "a long time coming." Matthew took great pains to deal with the effects of that wrong expectation; and so, as we shall see, did Luke, who, quite independently of Matthew, faced up to the same problems in revising the gospel of Mark.

WHO WROTE LUKE-ACTS, AND WHY DID SHE DO IT?

HAS ANYONE EVER NOTICED that in Luke-Acts, it is only *males* who fail to understand and believe the point of the resurrection and the delay of the *parousia*? Luke transforms the Markan theme of the obtuseness of the disciples into the rather different theme of the obtuseness of *male* disciples. The Gospel of Luke follows Mark's account in placing three women at the empty tomb; but whereas Mark writes that the women, on learning of the resurrection, "said nothing to anybody, for they were afraid" (Mark 16:8), Luke insists that, "returning from the tomb, they reported all this to the Eleven and all the others," but "the apostles," on hearing the report, remained obdurate: "the story appeared to them to be nonsense, and they would not believe them" (Luke 24:9, 11). In Luke, women are the first to believe and preach the resurrection faith. Matthew, like Luke, had refused to accept Mark's report that the women who found the empty tomb had said nothing to anybody, insisting instead that "they ran to tell the disciples" (Matt. 28:8); but in Matthew, the disciples believe the report, and faithfully set out for Galilee "to the mountain where Jesus had told them to meet him" (Matt. 28:16). Only Luke stresses the unique depth of female faith and understanding. Male disciples in Luke's work have just as much trouble grasping the reason for the delay of the *parousia* as they have accepting the resurrection. Even though Luke presents Jesus speaking perfectly clear parables about the great span of time between Crucifixion and Second Coming (the Untrustworthy Servant, who tells himself "The master is a long time coming" [Luke 12:44], and the Parable of the Talents, about a "man of noble birth [who] went on a long journey abroad, to have himself appointed king and then return," a parable spoken against those who "thought the kingdom of God might dawn at any moment" [Luke 19:11-12]), male Christians after the Resurrection, Luke writes, still could not understand. Just before Jesus' Ascension in Acts, "men of Galilee" (Acts 1:11) ask Jesus, "Lord, is this the time at which you are to restore sovereignty to Israel?" evoking Luke's statement of the main theme of the Book of Acts: the spread of Christianity to the "farthest corners of the earth" under the guidance of the Holy Spirit (Acts 1:8). This worldwide propagation of Christianity will begin, says Luke's resurrected Jesus, "within the next few days, [when] you will be baptized with the Holy Spirit" (Acts 1:5)—the events of Pentecost, which allow Luke to state the second greatest theme of Acts: that the Spirit-guided preaching of the gospel will be performed by *women* as well as men. At Pentecost, Luke has Peter quote the great words of the prophet Joel: "This will happen in the last days: I will pour out upon everyone a portion of my spirit; and your sons and daughters will prophesy...Yes, I will endue even my slaves, both men and women, with a portion of my spirit, and they shall prophesy" (Acts 2:17-18). This phrase, "both men and women," is central to all of Luke-Acts, as we shall see. The Gospel of Luke puts what might seem like a curious emphasis on female followers of Jesus, women who were not only his disciples, but actually the patrons of Jesus and the apostles:

> With him were the Twelve and a number of women who had been set free from evil spirits and infirmities: Mary, known as Mary of Magdala, from whom seven devils had come out, Joanna, the wife of Chuza a steward of Herod's, Susanna, and many others. These women provided for them out of their own resources. (Luke 8:2-3)

There is no parallel for this passage in any other gospel. Only Luke presents the surprising notion that Jesus' circle may have actually contained more women than men (twelve male apostles, three named and "many" [*pollai*] unnamed women), and the women were the financial support! Moreover, only Luke puts these female disciples on the scene when Jesus foretells his own death and resurrection, and only Luke presents them as understanding, under the prodding of an angel, what he had meant:

> "Remember what he told you while he was still in Galilee: how he must be given up

into the power of sinful men and be crucified, and must rise again on the third day."
Then they recalled his words and, returning from the tomb, they reported all this.
(Luke 24:7-8)

Luke shows an overwhelming interest in the role of women. In contrast
to Matthew, Luke has an angel announce to Mary rather than to Joseph
the Holy Spirit's role in the conception of Jesus (Matt. 1:20; Luke 1:26).
Indeed, writes Raymond Brown, "For Luke, Mary was a more important
figure than Joseph" (Brown, 1977, 130). Moreover, the first person to
receive the Holy Spirit and proclaim Jesus as "Lord" is a woman, Elizabeth
(Luke 1:43), the first person Jesus mentions in public is a woman, the
widow of Sarepta (Luke 4:26), the first person raised from the dead in Acts
is a woman, Tabitha (Acts 9:40), Paul's first convert in Europe is a woman,
Lydia (Acts 16:14), and Paul's first exorcism is of a woman, a slave in
Philippi (Acts 16:18). And this is only a brief selection of the very large
number of women who play important roles in Luke-Acts, a fact that
has not gone unnoticed by scholars. A common explanation has been that
Luke had a "desire to enhance the position of women in a male-dominated
society" as part of a program to "present Jesus' ministry to the oppressed
and excluded" (Tannehill, 1986, 132, 139). Feminist scholars have long
argued that in earliest Christianity women held major apostolic roles
while later generations attempted (successfully) to reassert patriarchal
authority: "While—for apologetic reasons—the post-Pauline and
post-Petrine writers seek to limit women's leadership roles in the Christian
community to roles which are culturally and religiously acceptable, the
evangelists called Mark and John highlight the alternative character of the
Christian community, and therefore accord women apostolic and minis-
terial leadership" (Schüssler Fiorenza, 1994, 334).

While Schüssler Fiorenza grants a kind of feminism to Mark and John,
she and other feminist scholars have felt more dubious, even conflicted,
about Luke. Turid Karlsen Seim, for example, reports "a remarkable diver-
gence in the present perception regarding the treatment of women by
Luke: Is Luke within the Christian Testament corpus a rare friend of
women reflecting equality and a radical revision of the role of women in

the early church? Or is his major contribution to impose the 'Lukan silence,' representing a programmatic androcentrism that pleads the subordination of women?" (1994, 728).

It certainly seems puzzling that while some have seen Luke as an early Christian feminist, others have seen Luke as an early Christian anti-feminist. That opinions about Luke can differ so radically is a sign of real complexity, of richly nuanced presentation, in the works of this great writer. The Lukan theme "both men and women" clearly calls for more subtle analysis.

We might begin with a suggestion of the feminist religious historian Ross Shepard Kraemer that "it is within the realm of possibility that the patron of Luke-Acts was in fact not a man named Theophilus, as Luke 1:3 and Acts 1:1 currently read, but a woman named Theophile" (1992, 233). The difference, in Greek, between the masculine and feminine endings of this name is only the difference between short e (*epsilon*) and long e (*eta*), "a frequent change in ancient manuscripts that could have occurred under numerous circumstances" (Kraemer, 1992, 233). That there might have been a female patron for Luke-Acts, says Kraemer, is "consistent with Luke's particular emphasis on female patrons" such as Joanna and Susanna in Luke 8 and Lydia in Acts 16. But even though feminist historians would be gratified to find a female first reader for Luke-Acts, Kraemer acknowledges that "there is no textual support for such a reading" (1992, 234).

But even if the addressee of Luke-Acts was a man after all and an Imperial official (Luke calls him *kratiste* ["most excellent"] *Theophile*), Kraemer is onto something, sensing a presence, a tone and a set of attitudes, that a male reader like myself would do well to consider. What if the female presence in Luke-Acts is *the author herself?* Any reader who makes this speculative leap will then find the textual evidence compelling. Luke's desire to "enhance the position of women in a male-dominated society" (Tannehill, 1986, 132) makes sense if Luke herself were a woman; then the strikingly large number of female characters central to the story of Luke-Acts leaps to the fore: Elizabeth, Mary, Anna, the widow of Sarepta,

IV: Who Wrote Luke-Acts, and Why Did She Do It?

LUKE'S INTENSE CONCERN FOR WOMEN
COMPARED TO THE OTHER GOSPEL WRITERS

• Angelic Annunciation of Jesus' conception made to Mary (Luke 1:31) rather than to Joseph (Matt. 1:20).

• Luke uses Greek word for "women" 11 times, Matt. 6 times, Mark twice, John none.

• Luke uses Greek word for "womb" 8 times, Matt. and John once, Mark none.

• Only Luke interested in Mary's inner life (2:18, 34, 51).

• Only Luke gives us the famous lines rejoicing in pregnancy: "My soul doth magnify the Lord" (1:46); "'Blessed art thou among women and blessed is the fruit of thy womb" (1:42).

• Only biblical author to mention fetal quickening and to describe it as evoking visitation of Holy Spirit (1:41).

• Only Evangelist to imply that Jesus' female intimates outnumbered his male (8:2).

• Only Evangelist to imply that Jesus and the Twelve were financed by women (8:3).

• First to call Jesus "Lord" is a woman in Luke (1:43).

• First person resurrected after Jesus is a woman, says Luke (Acts 9:40).

• First European Christian is a woman, says Luke (Acts 11).

• Only New Testament writer to insist that though women were the first to believe and preach the resurrection faith, male disciples refused to believe (24:10-11).

• Only New Testament writer to stress that "both men and women" shall prophesy (Acts 2:18).

• Only Evangelist to cite a "prophetess, Anna" (Luke 2:36).

• Only biblical author interested in female osteoporosis (Luke 13:10-13).

• Only Evangelist to praise women who "spoke up" to men (1:60) and dubiously questioned an angel (1:34).

• Luke gives us the largest cast of female characters in the New Testament.

the widow of Nain, Joanna, Susanna, Mary Magdalene, the "sinner" with the bottle of myrrh, Mary and Martha, the woman who lost a coin, the widow who importuned the unjust judge, the Queen of Sheba, Mary the mother of James, John Mark's mother, Sapphira, Rhoda, Lydia, Tabitha, Damaris, Priscilla, Philip's four daughters, Paul's sister, Drusilla, Bernice; the list is surprisingly long. Merely in terms of words and names, Luke has an overwhelmingly greater interest in women than does any other New Testament writer. The Gospel of Luke uses the Greek word for "women" eleven times, Matthew six times, Mark two, John none. Luke uses the Greek word for "womb" eight times, Matthew and John once each, Mark not at all. Luke uses the Greek word for "widow" seven times, Mark twice, the others once. Only Luke uses the plural "widows." I speculate that there was a personal reason for Luke's special interest in women and widows: Luke was herself a Gentile Christian widow in the same position as the Gentile widow of Sarepta who is the subject of Jesus' very first public speech (Luke 4:26)—bereft of an only son, just like the widow of Nain.

More than any other New Testament writer, Luke concerns herself with the inner lives of women. Far more interested in Mary than in Joseph, Luke twice gives us Mary's inner thoughts about her son: after the shepherds came to the manger, she "treasured up all these things and pondered over them" (Luke 2:18), and after Jesus at age twelve was found in the Temple astounding the teachers there, Mary "treasured up all these things in her heart" (Luke 2:51). Even the emotional impact of fetal quickening is of special concern to Luke—the only biblical author, I suggest, who had personally felt it—for when pregnant Mary visits pregnant Elizabeth, "when Elizabeth heard Mary's greeting, the baby stirred in her womb. Then Elizabeth was filled with the Holy Spirit and cried aloud" (Luke 1:41). That fetal quickening should precede a visitation of the Holy Spirit is unique to Luke in all of Scripture, and grants Elizabeth the insight to be first to call Jesus "Lord" (Luke 1:43).

This concern for the inner lives of women extends with special intensity toward women whose children die. When Jesus saw the widow of Nain, bereft of an only son, "his heart went out to her" (Luke 7:13). And remember that Elizabeth and Mary, who between them utter the most famous lines of poetry on earth that rejoice in pregnancy ("Blessed art thou among women and blessed is the fruit of thy womb"; "My soul doth magnify the Lord..."), both do so with Luke's knowledge of their sons' coming executions; the joy of both women is rich with dramatic irony. Luke herself, I speculate, had experienced the death of a beloved son. Mary's future grief is spotlighted by the prophet Simeon on the day of the baby Jesus' presentation at the Temple, when he tells Mary that "This child is destined to be a sign which men reject; and you too shall be pierced to the heart" (Luke 2:34). Nowhere in Scripture outside Luke-Acts is there so much concern for maternal emotion.

Indeed, Luke had searched the Old Testament for its few passages of maternal joy, and used them as the basis for her own stories of Elizabeth and Mary: Mary's surpassingly beautiful *Magnificat* (Luke 1:46-55) is closely modeled on Hannah's prayer of thanksgiving after the birth of her son Samuel (I Sam. 2:1-10), while the entire account of Elizabeth's long-delayed and divinely-foretold conception of John the Baptist is modeled after Hannah's parallel story in I Samuel chapter one.

This concern for maternal emotion is part of Luke's strong sympathetic identification with those who must endure the death of an only child; Luke will even change her source to make that point. For when in Mark's Gospel Jairus comes to Jesus to plead with him, "My little daughter is at death's door" (Mark 5:23), Luke in her version of this story changes "little daughter" to "only daughter" (Luke 8:42), a change made deliberately to balance Luke's account in the previous chapter of Jesus' Resurrection of the "only son" of the widow of Nain (Luke 7:12). And as I shall argue, Luke herself wrote that last story, basing it on the account of Elijah's reviving of the son of the widow of Sarepta in I Kings.

Luke's special concern for mothers who have lost a child extends with special intensity to "widows in the full sense,...alone in the world" (I Tim. 5:5)—those who have lost both husband *and* children, and with equal intensity to *Gentile* widows like Luke herself. In Jesus' first public speech in the Gospel of Luke, he announces in advance a theme central to the Book of Acts—the Christian mission to non-Jews—by invoking the story of the Gentile widow of Sarepta in I Kings 17: "There were many widows in Israel, you may be sure, in Elijah's time, when for three years and six months the skies never opened, and famine lay hard over the whole country; yet it was to none of those that Elijah was sent, but to a widow of Sarepta in the territory of Sidon" (Luke 4:25-26). This speech, found only in Luke's Gospel, is just her first use of the widow of Sarepta's story; we know that Luke meditated long and lovingly on this narrative, finding special meaning in it, for it also became the basis for her beautiful narrative about the widow of Nain, a story again found only in Luke's Gospel.

If Luke found in the story of the Sidonian widow of Sarepta an image of her own condition, we can understand why stories of the death of an only son held such poignancy for her, and why hope of his resurrection lay at the heart of her faith. Luke's story of the widow of Nain is modeled directly on the story of the widow of Sarepta, which Luke read in the Greek Septuagint version, repeating key words of its vocabulary:

> And it came to pass that the word of the Lord came to Eliu, saying, "Arise, and go to Sarepta of the Sidonian land: I have there commanded a widow-woman to maintain thee." And he arose and went to Sarepta, and came to the gate of the city....
>
> And it came to pass afterward, that the son of the woman, the mistress of the house, was sick; and his sickness was very severe, until there was no breath left in him....And Eliu said to the woman, "Give me thy son." And he took him out of her bosom,...and called on the Lord, and said, "O Lord, my God, let, I pray thee, the soul of this child return unto him." And it was so, and the child cried out, and he brought him down from the upper chamber into the house, and gave him to his mother. (III Kings 17:8-10, 19-23 LXX)
>
> Afterwards Jesus went to a town called Nain, accompanied by his disciples and a large crowd. As he approached the gate of the town he met a funeral. The dead man was the only son of his widowed mother; and many of the townspeople were there with her. When the Lord saw her his heart went out to her, and he said, "Weep no more." With that he stepped forward and laid his hand on the bier; and the bearers halted. Then he spoke: "Young man, rise up!" The dead man sat up, and began to speak; and Jesus gave him back to his mother. (Luke 7:11-15)

IV: Who Wrote Luke-Acts, and Why Did She Do It?

Luke begins her story with the same words as her biblical model, "*Kai egeneto*" ("And it came to pass"). Luke's story, like its model, concerned the raising of the son of a widow (*chēra*). Luke's Jesus, like Elijah, "went" (*eporeuthē*) on his mission to the town, encountering the widow "at the gate of the town" (*ton pylona tēs poleōs* in the Septuagint; *tē pylē tēs poleōs* in Luke). Following the model of Elijah, Luke has Jesus speak, touch the dead son, who then rises and speaks. And Luke concludes with exactly the same words as her model, "And he gave him to his mother" (*kai edōken auton tē mētri autou*). These last words seem to have special significance in Luke's own religious hopes.

If Luke was herself a Greek-speaking widow writing a history of earliest Christianity, then we can understand her pleasure in presenting the wonderfully ironic notion that it was Greek-speaking widows who were indirectly responsible for the spread of the Christian message out from Jerusalem in unexpected fulfillment of Jesus' final commission to "bear witness for me…to the ends of the earth" (Acts 1:8). Ironically this outreach begins in early Christian neglect of Greek-speaking widows in Jerusalem: "there was disagreement between those of them who spoke Greek and those who spoke the language of the Jews. The former party complained that their widows were being overlooked in the daily distribution" (Acts 6:1).

Stephen, along with others, is appointed to ensure a fair distribution, and he quickly rises to prominence. Soon he is accused of "blasphemous statements" and stoned to death (Acts 6:8). "This was," says Luke, "the beginning of a time of violent persecution for the church in Jerusalem," and the Christians were "scattered over the country districts of Judaea and Samaria," "preaching the Word" (Acts 8:1, 4). Luke's interest in the irony of Greek-speaking Christian widows' responsibility for world evangelizing seems an expression of her own status.

Luke's first example of an inspired widow who spreads the word about Jesus is the "prophetess, Anna," whom Luke deliberately pairs with the prophet Simeon in rejoicing at the presentation of the baby Jesus at the Temple. Peter's announcement that "both men and women…shall prophesy"

(Acts 2:18) finds its first fulfillment a generation before he speaks, when, after Simeon is heard rejoicing that Jesus will be for "all the nations" (Luke 2:31), we learn that

> There was also a prophetess, Anna the daughter of Phanuel, of the tribe of Asher. She was a very old woman, who had lived seven years with her husband after she was first married, and then alone as a widow to the age of eighty-four. She never left the temple, but worshipped day and night, fasting and praying. Coming up at that very moment, she returned thanks to God; and she talked about the child to all who were looking for the liberation of Jerusalem. (Luke 2:36-38)

Why does Luke show a woman expanding on what a man has already said? This tactic appears to be the first example of a recurrent pattern in Luke-Acts, what Robert Tannehill calls Luke's "tendency toward doubling, one version referring to a man and the other to a woman, resulting in male-female pairs" (1986, 132). But in Luke's account of Anna there is even more at work, for her description of this widowed prophetess sounds very much like a response to the kind of early Christian patronizing of women found in the First Letter to Timothy, which commands that "The status of widow is to be granted only to widows who are such in the full sense," those who have "no children or grandchildren." Such a widow should not be "given over to self-indulgence," but should be one who "attends the meetings for prayer and worship night and day [*deēsesin kai tais proseuchais nuktos kai hēmeras*]" (I Tim. 5:4-5). Anna, too, never left the temple in her supplications, worshipping night and day (*deēsesin latreuousa nukta kai hēmeran* (Luke 2:37); but Luke presents Anna flagrantly violating the rule in I Timothy: "I do not permit a woman to be a teacher,...she should be quiet" (I Tim. 2:12). Anna, we know, "talked about the child to all" (Luke 2:38), in fulfillment of Luke's theme that "both men and women" should prophesy.

Luke's tendency toward doubling, presenting male-female pairs, is clearly evident in the speeches of Jesus, as in Luke's version of the "Sign of Jonah":

> the only sign that will be given it is the sign of Jonah. For just as Jonah was a sign to the

Ninevites, so will the Son of Man be to this generation. At the Judgment, when the men of this generation are on trial, the Queen of the South will appear against them and ensure their condemnation, for she came from the ends of the earth to hear the wisdom of Solomon; and what is here is greater than Solomon. The men of Ninevah will appear at the Judgment when this generation is on trial, for they repented at the preaching of Jonah; and what is here is greater than Jonah. (Luke 11:30-32)

Although the Queen of the South has nothing to do with Jonah or the Ninevites to whom he preached, Luke nonetheless sees to it that the Sign of Jonah saying includes a woman, and a "believing" one at that. And notice that it was a woman who came from "the ends of the earth" to hear Solomon, an early foreshadowing of the commission to "both men and women."

In her reports of the sayings of Jesus, Luke sometimes seems to be making a sly feminist joke, as in her version of this saying from source Q shared with Matthew: "I tell you, on that night there will be two men in one bed; one will be taken, the other left. There will be two women together grinding corn: one will be taken, the other left" (Luke 17:34-35). This is subtly different from Matthew's version: "Then there will be two men in the field; one will be taken, the other left; two women grinding at the mill; one will be taken, the other left" (Matt. 24:40-41). It is typical of Luke's sense of humor to show the men in bed while the women work.

Luke's sense of humor is most apparent in the pair of parables found only in her gospel, another male/female pair, the Widow and the Unjust Judge placed next to the Pharisee and the Tax Collector. Perhaps the most masterful example of comic dramatic irony in the Bible stands in the second of these parables, where the Pharisee intones "I thank thee, O God, that I am not like the rest of men, greedy, dishonest, adulterous," in contrast to the tax-collector, who can only smite his breast and say "God have mercy on me, a sinner" (Luke 18:11, 13). Both men are praying in faith, but the one who thinks he condemns himself in fact acquits himself, while the other who rejoices in his virtue only condemns himself. Some persistence in prayer is of dubious value, says Luke in this parable, unless one is like the widow in its companion, who "constantly came before" a judge who "cared nothing for God or man," "demanding justice." "For a long time he refused; but in the end he said to himself, 'True, I care nothing for God or man: but this widow is so great a nuisance that I will see her righted before she wears me out with her persistence'" (Luke 18:3-5).

We all stand before God as bereft widows, and we need to speak up. Indeed the irony of a woman speaking up out of place and being reward-ed with blessing finds strong statement in the paired annunciation scenes to Zechariah, about to become father to John the Baptist, and to Mary, about to conceive Jesus. When the angel Gabriel appears to Zechariah to tell him that "Elizabeth will bear you a son," he answers dubiously, "How can I be sure of this? I am an old man and my wife is well on in years." His doubt angers the angel, who severely punishes him: "you will lose your power of speech, and remain silent until the day when these things hap-pen to you, because you have not believed me" (Luke 1:13, 18, 20).

In the parallel Annunciation to Mary, she answers Gabriel just as dubi-ously (and with much less reason to doubt that she might soon conceive, being on the eve of marriage to Joseph): "How can this be? I am still a virgin." But this time the angel answers patiently, explaining that "The Holy Spirit will come upon you" (Luke 1:34-35). A questioning woman who speaks up is rewarded with the blessing of the Holy Spirit—a theme continued in the story of Mary's kinswoman Elizabeth. When John the Baptist is born, "they were going to name him Zechariah after his father. But his mother spoke up and said. 'No! he is to be called John.'" But of course Zechariah is still mute and could not have told Elizabeth of Gabriel's instruction to call the child John (Luke 1:13, 60); her insight is miraculous and follows upon her "speaking up" as a mere woman was not supposed to do.

Luke's pairing of male/female stories continues with her determination to present activities of Jesus that show his saving interest for women as well as for men. As we have already seen, Luke deliberately pairs the story of the resurrection of Jairus' daughter (taken from Mark) with the new story (unique to Luke) of the widow of Nain's son. Another striking example of such pairing stands in chapters 13 and 14, healings on the Sabbath of a woman and a man. Luke begins the two stories with deliberate parallelism: "And behold, there was a woman" (*kai idou gynē*); "And behold, there was a man" (*kai idou anthropos*) (Luke 13:11; 14:2). Both stories are unique to Luke; and though she gives rather short shrift to the healing of the man— "he took the man, cured him, and sent him away" (Luke 14:4)—Luke dwells at some length on the healing of the woman, who appears to have a very serious case of osteoporosis, an illness much more common among women than among men:

> One Sabbath he was teaching in a synagogue, and there was a woman there possessed by a spirit of infirmity that had crippled her for eighteen years. She was bent double and quite unable to stand up straight. When Jesus saw her he called to her and said, "You are rid of your trouble." Then he laid his hands upon her, and at once she straightened up and began to praise God. (Luke 13:10-13)

Women were, of course, required to keep silent in synagogues; this story bears the hallmarks of Luke's own creation. That the woman was "bent double" (*synkuptousa*) and quite unable to "stand up straight" (*anakupsai*) is a sign of Luke's own hand, since the first Greek word above appears nowhere else in the New Testament, while the second appears again only at Luke 21:28. And when the president of the synagogue is "indignant with Jesus for healing on the Sabbath," Jesus berates him as a hypocrite, for who would not "loose his ox or his donkey from the manger to take it out to water on the Sabbath? And here is this woman, a daughter of Abraham, who has been kept prisoner…" (Luke 13:15-16). Again, "daughter of Abraham" is a phrase unique to Luke.

Luke not only cites male-female pairs who are worthy of healing, she also pairs those worthy of death. In Acts, after Ananias sold some property and promised the money to the church, he deliberately withheld part of it. Peter saw through his ruse, and when he publicly berated Ananias, "he dropped dead; and all the others who heard were awestruck" (Acts 5:5). Luke's point about lying and greed is well and clearly made; but she also wishes to stress that wives are equally responsible with their husbands for support of the church and for holding to the truth; wives are not just passive participants in Christianity. Since it was with the "full knowledge of his wife that [Ananias] kept back part of the purchase-money," when three hours later she enters and is berated by Peter, Sapphira too "dropped dead at his feet" (Acts 5:10).

For Luke, women must have a large and responsible role even in the financial affairs of the church. Luke in fact opposed the patriarchal notion expressed in I Timothy 2:15 that women "will be saved by childbearing," for she gives us a saying of Jesus to the contrary: "While he was speaking thus, a woman in the crowd called out, 'Happy is the womb that carried you and the breasts that suckled you!' He rejoined, 'No, happy are those who hear the word of God and keep it'" (Luke 11:27-28). Luke stresses more than any other New Testament writer that women too have important roles in following Jesus; their salvation comes not just from childbearing, important as that is. Luke argues throughout her two books that women have other great duties beyond "women's work"; indeed she would have personal reason for knowing the never-ending nature of the duties traditionally assigned to women, and that these can be meaningfully neglected. Only Luke tells the story of Mary and Martha:

> Jesus came to a village where a woman named Martha made him welcome in her home. She had a sister, Mary, who seated herself at the Lord's feet and stayed there listening to his words. Now Martha was distracted by her many tasks, so she came to him and said, "Lord, do you not care that my sister has left me to get on with the work by myself? Tell her to come and lend a hand." But the Lord answered, "Martha, Martha, you are fretting and fussing about so many things; but one thing is necessary. The part that Mary has chosen is best." (Luke 10:38-42)

Martha acts as head of household, since she and her sister are unmarried, and, like other strong Lukan females, does the unthinkable: inviting a man into her home and engaging in dialogue with him. In this she is like Elizabeth who "spoke up," like Jesus' mother who dubiously questioned an angel, like Lydia, another unmarried woman, who "insisted" that Paul stay with her in her home (Acts 16:15). Martha fulfills the role of her name ("Lady" or "Mistress" in Aramaic). She is in fact the fourth woman in the

IV: Who Wrote Luke-Acts, and Why Did She Do It?

Gospel of Luke whose activities are described with forms of the word "deacon": Mary Magdalene, Joanna and Susanna "provided" (*diēkonoun*) for Jesus and the Twelve; Martha was distracted by her "tasks" (*diakonian*) and complained that Mary left her to do all the "work" (*diakonein*). That women were deacons in early Christianity is confirmed by Paul, who names Phoebe as *diakonon* of the church in Cenchreae (Rom. 16:1). In other words, Luke reads the organization of Jesus' own intimate circle as a model for church life of her own time, as we shall see in the next chapter, on the Book of Acts, where women assume leadership roles in house-churches. But Luke performs a double irony with Mary and Martha: 1. that a woman should assume a leadership role as a deacon, but 2. that there is something even more important than a leader, namely a follower of Jesus. The story of Mary and Martha does not denigrate "women's work," but rather stresses that even church leaders (and even when they are women!) are called to be disciples first. Indeed, "Martha, Martha" may be a call to discipleship like "Saul, Saul" (Acts 9:4), rather than a rebuke. And, finally, notice that Luke in this story does not distinguish between male and female roles, but between two different ways women can be Christians, as deacon and disciple (for Mary's sitting at Jesus' feet marked her as disciple).

Luke, in other words, consistently and deliberately presents female as well as male disciples; indeed she is the only author of New Testament narrative to use the feminine form (*mathētria*) of the Greek word for disciple, in her story about Dorcas, who was so important to the church at Joppa that Peter was called in to resurrect her when she died, in Acts chapter 9. For Luke, "man and woman stand together side by side before God. They are equal in honor and grace; they are endowed with the same gifts and have the same responsibilities" (Flender, 1967, 10). Clearly, in some sense or another, Luke's theme "both men and women" marks her as an early Christian feminist. Now remember her historical context: an exact contemporary of Luke was the author of Revelation, who wrote that those "who alone from the world had been ransomed" were 144,000 "men who did not defile themselves with women, for they are virgins" (Rev. 14:3, 4).

Misogyny was the essence of apocalyptic Christianity in Luke's time and even a generation before, when Paul declared that "It is a good thing for a man to have nothing to do with women" (I Cor. 7:1). Implicit in Luke-Acts is an attack upon misogynistic apocalyptic Christianity; that "both men and women" have key roles in the extended period between Ascension and Second Coming is among the central themes of Luke's work. Was there a Christian man alive at the end of the first century capable of writing two volumes on this question?

❧ V ❧

Luke: Her Mind and Art

LUKE GIVES US ONE OF THE MOST REMARKABLE STATEMENTS of authorial method in the entire New Testament:

> The author to Theophilus: Many writers have undertaken to draw up an account of the events that have taken place among us, following the traditions handed down to us by the original eyewitnesses and servants of the Gospel. And so I in my turn, your Excellency, as one who has gone over the whole course of these events in detail, have decided to write a connected narrative for you, so as to give you authentic knowledge about the matters of which you have been informed. (Luke 1:1-4)

This is a very revealing passage. Luke admits that she is not an eyewitness of Jesus, but is rather an interpreter of earlier material. She also has highly mixed feelings about this material: though she believes it comes from the time of eyewitnesses, it still does not satisfy her criterion of "authentic knowledge" but rather needs her correction and revision. Luke's own work would be superfluous if those "many" other writers she has consulted had done the job adequately; but they have not, so she does it all again, going "over the whole course of these events in detail."

Modern scholars have identified two of Luke's "many" sources: the Gospel of Mark and a hypothetical document called "Q" (from German *Quelle*, "source"), an identification now known as the "two-source theory": "Luke's primary sources are the same as those of Matthew, i.e., the Gospel of Mark and the Synoptic Sayings Source [Q]" (Koester, 1990, 336). Indeed Luke had good reason to feel uneasy about Mark. She possessed an anonymous copy of this document, thinking, wrongly, that it was based on eyewitness testimony about Jesus, but sensing grave incompetence in its composition—so much so that she rejected about half of it (unlike Matthew, who uses ninety percent of Mark, Luke repeats only about fifty percent).

A good example of what Luke would have regarded as the ineptness of Mark and his use of the Bible will appear in a comparison of the openings of their baptism accounts in Mark 1 and Luke 3. Like Mark, Luke regarded Isaiah 40:3 ("A voice crying aloud in the wilderness") as being "really" a statement about John the Baptist, but Luke is much more knowledgeable about the Septuagint Bible than Mark—indeed, Luke probably grew up as a "God-fearing" Greek-speaking Gentile, reading all her life the Greek version of the Hebrew Bible, whereas Mark seems to have been an adult convert to Christianity from paganism, and was rather less familiar with the Septuagint. Mark does not know, as I showed earlier, that the passage he quotes as from Isaiah is in fact a garbled combination of Malachi 3:1 and Exodus 23:20 joined with Isaiah 40:3; Luke, in reproducing the passage from Mark, drops the words not found in Isaiah. Moreover, Mark did not go back to the text of Isaiah, as did Luke, and read the entire passage to understand its full implication; Luke did, and quoted not just verse 3 of Isaiah 40, but verses 4 and 5 as well, to get to the great universalist statement that is central to her own vision of Christianity: "A voice crying aloud in the wilderness, 'Prepare a way for the Lord; clear a straight path for him. Every ravine shall be filled in, and every mountain and hill leveled; the corners shall be straightened, and the rugged ways made smooth; and all flesh shall see God's deliverance'" (Luke 3:4-6).

After the argument of my preceding chapter, we can grasp that for Luke, "all flesh" means not just Gentiles as well as Jews, it means women as well as men. Luke's implicit argument in her use of Mark 1 is that Mark does not even understand the real point of the passage in Isaiah he inaccurately and incompletely cites.

Deleting half of Mark gives room not only for the Q material, but also for a large body of uniquely Lukan material—what scholars have called "source L": "Like Matthew, Luke employs additional materials not drawn from" either Mark or Q. "Most of these are usually assigned to a third source used by Luke ('L')" (Koester, 1990, 336). We can view "source L" as a shorthand term for verses found only in Luke, which are thus strongly revealing of her mind and art; and the first thing to note about "L" is that it has a much higher percentage of material about women than we find in any other gospel. Luke supplements Mark with stories that are in a sense about herself. Of the four healing miracles Luke adds to Mark, two are for the benefit of women: the raising of the only son of the widow of Nain (7:7-17), the healing of the woman with the spirit of infirmity (13:10-17), the healing of the man with dropsy (14:1-6), and the healing of the ten lepers (17:11-19). From "source L" Luke adds to Mark eight "Apophthegmata" ("sayings of Jesus set in a brief context"—Bultmann's term [*Synoptic*, 11]); half of these concern women: the woman who was a sinner (7:36-50), the women who provided for Jesus from their own resources (8:1-3), Mary and Martha (10:38-42), the blessedness of Jesus' mother (11:24-26), dividing the inheritance (11:24-26), the call for repentance (13:1-5), Jesus' answer to Herod (13:31-33), and the story of short Zacchaeus (19:1-10). In each case, Luke balances material about men and women equally, and in each group, puts the women first. This chapter will be a study of those parts of "source L" (and its continuation in the Book of Acts) that tell us about the gender and mind of the author of Luke-Acts.

Biblical scholars have increasingly come to use this hyphenated title, recognizing the importance of the two-volume structure of Luke-Acts; as Luke Timothy Johnson has written, "The decision to read these separate texts as a single literary work represents the triumph of a literary critical approach to the NT writings, concerned less for the historical data contained in a writing, or the prehistory of its discrete parts, than with its distinctive voice" (*ABD* IV, 104).

Johnson goes on to argue that to be concerned with Luke's "voice" as an author and to "adopt the category 'Luke-Acts,'" "means to accept a contemporary literary designation in preference to the traditional perception of the texts"; the implications of this "literary" view of Luke-Acts, says Johnson, "have only begun to be developed," for readers are still learning to grasp that "Luke is above all a gifted story-teller" (*ABD* IV, 105). I would add only one term to Johnson's description: Luke is a gifted *female* story-teller.

Luke as story-teller does not name most of her sources of information, since they are anonymous to her; she possessed both Mark and Q as anonymous documents, trustworthy in that they came down from the time of "eyewitnesses," yet still not sufficiently "authentic." There is, however, one important source that Luke does name and identify, and it is basic to "source L"—the Greek Septuagint version of the Hebrew Bible, which Luke calls "the scriptures" (Luke 24:27). This text will be a major source for Luke of information about both Jesus and the early church. She begins to explain this method in the first verse of her gospel with her unusual term for the events "that have taken place" among us (*peplērophorēmenōn*—literally, "having been fulfilled"). This is the first of Luke's uses of the "divine passive," the passive voice employed to indicate divine action. The "fulfillment" of biblical prophecy in the life of Jesus (Luke) and in the early church (Acts) is a key theme in this two-volume work. In one "L" episode, for example, the apparition of the resurrected Jesus on the road to Emmaus, Luke has Jesus explain from "Moses and all the prophets" "the passages which referred to himself in every part of the scriptures" (Luke 24:27).

To Luke, "the scriptures" meant the Septuagint, one of her most important sources of information about Jesus and the early church. Or, to put it another way, Luke will frequently correct and supplement the (often, to her, inadequate) information in the "many writers" she has "gone over in detail" whose accounts are still not "authentic" enough, with another source of divinely guaranteed accuracy, the Hebrew Bible in its Greek version, which was as she read it really a book about Jesus; for as Jesus had said, "all the scriptures" contained "passages which referred to himself." I shall argue that "source L" (and its continuation in the Book of Acts) is in many cases the Greek Septuagint Bible refracted through Luke's creative imagination as new stories about Jesus and the early church. In these cases, "L" material will then of course be extremely revealing about Luke herself; there will be rather more in them of Luke than of Jesus or Peter or Paul, and a great deal about Luke's two great themes, "both Jews and Gentiles," "both men and women."

V: Luke: Her Mind and Art

After the baptism scene in Luke, the next "L" passage is Jesus' maiden speech, at his hometown of Nazareth. Here, Luke has Jesus name the biblical precedents for his shocking ministry to Gentiles and women, in words that "infuriated" the Nazarenes, who "threw him out of the town" (Luke 4:29), and name, in the process, the biblical sources of two of the miracle stories in Luke that come from "source L": "There were many widows in Israel, you may be sure, in Elijah's time…yet it was to none of these that Elijah was sent, but to a widow at Sarepta in the territory of Sidon. Again, in the time of the prophet Elisha, there were many lepers in Israel, and not one of them was healed, but only Naaman, the Syrian."(Luke 4:25-27).

Thus Jesus' first speech stresses Luke's major theme, that the gospel is for women and Gentiles as well as "men of Israel," while at the same time preparing the reader for two miracle stories found only in Luke: the raising of the son of the widow of Nain (which Luke based on the story of the widow of Sarepta, as I showed above), and the healing of the ten lepers (based in part on the story of Naaman, as I show below). That the second of these is a prime example of Luke's story-telling abilities has long been suspected; Bultmann observed many years ago that in the healing of the ten lepers, "Mk. 1:40-45 has been transposed into an imaginary story" (Bultmann, 1976, 240):

> Once he was approached by a leper, who knelt before him begging his help. "If only you will," said the man, "you can cleanse me." Moved to compassion, Jesus stretched out his hand, touched him, and said, "Indeed I will; be clean again." The leprosy left him immediately, and he was clean. Then he dismissed him with this stern warning: "be sure you say nothing to anybody. Go and show yourself to the priest, and make the offering laid down by Moses for your cleansing; that will certify the cure." (Mark 1:40-45)

Luke had already used this story nearly word-for-word in 5:12-16, but she needs it one more time to "fulfill" the healing of the leprous Naaman, whom Jesus had mentioned in his maiden speech, and she does so by combining the above account from Mark 1 with the story of Naaman in Septuagint IV Kings. Here is Luke's brilliant creation about yet another good Samaritan:

In the course of his journey to Jerusalem, he was traveling through the midst of Samaria and Galilee. As he was entering a village, he was met by ten men with leprosy. They stood some way off and called out to him, "Jesus, Master, take pity on us." When he saw them he said, "Go and show yourself to the priests"; and while they were on their way, they were made clean. One of them, finding himself cured, turned back praising God aloud. He threw himself down at Jesus' feet and thanked him. And he was a Samaritan. (Luke 17:11-16)

The opening of this story is clearly Luke's own invention, since there is no such place as the "midst of Samaria and Galilee" (*meson Samarias kai Galilaias*); Luke needs to indicate that the ten lepers are some of them Galilean, some Samaritan. Since there is no such area, the village must also be unnamed, being as imaginary as the province. And Luke has forgotten that Jews and Samaritans hated each other so much, even the lepers of the two groups would not remain together. At least one of the ten lepers is a Samaritan, and here the story betrays its origin in Mark 1:44 ("Go and show yourself to the priest"): what would a Jewish priest do for a Samaritan, and why would a Samaritan go to a Jewish priest? For once, Luke uses Mark uncritically. The setting and other details come from the story of Elisha's healing of leprous Naaman in Septuagint IV Kings, a story Luke has already highlighted in Jesus' maiden speech as basic to her themes. Naaman the Syrian is healed in Samaria, the source for Luke's setting of her version. Elisha tells Naaman to "go" (*poreutheis*) wash in the Jordan, and "be cleansed" (*katharisthese*) (IV Kings 5:15 LXX), just as Jesus tells the ten lepers to "go" (*poreuthentes*) to the priests, and on the way they were "made clean" (*ekatharisthesan*). One of the lepers "turned back" (*hypestrepsen*) after his cleansing to praise God, just as Naaman "returned" (*epestrepse*) to Elisha to praise God after his cleansing (IV Kings 5:15 LXX).

Luke's special concern for stricken non-Jews parallels her special concern for stricken widows, as is shown in the other story Luke prepares us for in that maiden speech of Jesus at Nazareth, as the widow of Sarepta becomes for her the model for the widow of Nain, women whose sons were brought back to life. I showed already in the last chapter how the

Nain story is based on the one set at Sarepta; now I need only add that Luke's story bears in its vocabulary the marks of her own composition and does not seem to come from Christian tradition. Luke's account of the widow of Nain begins with the word "Afterwards" (*en tō hexēs*), a construction used only in Luke-Acts. At the city gate, Jesus saw a dead man "being carried out" (*exekomizeto*). Only here in the New Testament do we find this word. And when Jesus laid his hand on "the bier" (*tēs sorou*), Luke again is the only user of this word in the New Testament. After Jesus speaks to the young man, "he sat up" (*anekathisen*), a word used only here and in Acts 9:40. This story seems to bear Luke's own signature.

To the extent that stories from "source L" are in fact Luke's creations from the Septuagint or other sources, it could be said that "L" is also a "source" for stories in the Book of Acts. That Luke was a great "story-teller" applies also to some of her accounts about Peter and Paul.

Luke actually knew very little about Peter aside from what Mark's Gospel told her, and not much more about Paul; they were both figures of legend for her, but she as story-teller had central roles for them in the Book of Acts. As I noted in the previous chapter, two of the main themes in Acts are "both Jews and Gentiles" and "both men and women." Peter and Paul are the figures who carry the brunt of these themes in Acts. That Luke invents her own vision of Peter is clear from Acts 15:10, where she has Peter call the Mosaic Law "a yoke which neither we nor our fathers were able to bear." This is not the historical Peter known to Paul in his Letter to the Galatians, where Paul writes that he had to berate Peter publicly for refusing to take "his meals with gentile Christians...because he was afraid of the advocates of circumcision" who insisted that Jewish Christians like Peter continue the Jewish practice of non-association with gentiles (Gal. 2:12). Again, in the same chapter of Acts, Luke has Peter declare that "God...ordained that from my lips the Gentiles should hear and believe the message of the Gospel" (Acts 15:7). This is not the historical Peter, for Paul declares to the Galatians that the meeting described by Luke in Acts 15 actually determined that "I had been entrusted with the Gospel for Gentiles as surely as Peter had been entrusted with the Gospel for Jews" (Gal. 2:7).

Luke's Paul is likewise to a considerable extent her fictional creation. She had not read (and never quotes) any of Paul's letters and knew very little about his theology or life; for example, she shows him in Acts going off to Jerusalem almost immediately after his conversion, where Barnabas introduced him to "the apostles" (Acts 9:27), whereas Paul swears in Galatians that it was "three years" after his conversion before he went up to Jerusalem, and then he met only Cephas and James, "and not any other of the apostles" (Gal. 1:18-19). But Luke had determined that in Acts, just as Peter was to be the first apostle to bring the gospel to a Gentile man, Cornelius, so Paul was to be the first one to bring the gospel to a Gentile woman, Lydia—one more example of Luke's male/female pairings of narratives; and both stories are Luke's own magnificent fictional creations. And as Peter was to be the apostle to resurrect a Jewish Christian woman in Acts—Tabitha/Dorcas—so Paul would be the apostle to resurrect a gentile male—Eutychus. And again, both stories are Luke's own creations.

Central to Luke-Acts is the certainty that Christianity is destined for "all flesh"—Jew and Gentile, male and female. Luke grants to Peter the honor of baptizing the first Gentile, Cornelius, though Peter must first be prepared to associate with a non-Jew (thus becoming ritually unclean) by a heavenly vision, a story Luke composed out of Septuagint Ezekiel. As a prelude to his prophetic role, Ezekiel has a series of visions; in the first, "the heavens opened" [*ēnoichthēsan hoi ouranoi*] (Ezek. 1:1 LXX). Peter, about to receive his prophetic commission to go to the Gentile Cornelius, also sees in a vision that "heaven opened" [*ton ouranon aneōgmenon*] (Acts 10:11). In his next vision, Ezekiel is shown something and told to "eat" [*phage*] (Ezek. 2:9 LXX). Peter too in his vision is shown something and told to "eat" [*phage*] (Acts 10:13). Ezekiel is told to eat unclean food, bread baked with human dung, but the prophet, in shocked horror, demurs, "By no means, Lord" [*mēdamos Kyrie*] (Ezek. 4:14 LXX), just as Peter is told in his vision to eat unclean food, and likewise demurs, "By no means, Lord" [*Mēdamos kyrie*] (Acts 10:14). Ezekiel declares that he has never touched any "uncleanness" [*akatharsia*] (Ezek. 4:14 LXX), just as Peter declares that he too has never eaten anything "unclean" [*akatharton*] (Acts 10:14). Peter, finally understanding that the vision means he should call no one unclean, is thus prepared to associate, as a fellow Christian, with the Gentile Cornelius. Luke believed that the prophecy of Ezekiel was, like the rest of the scriptures, written "with foreknowledge of the Messiah" and of the Christian mission "to the ends of the earth" (Acts 2:31; 1:8); thus Ezekiel's visions "really" were, in a sense, Peter's in advance.

Given Luke's pattern of male/female pairs, if Peter is to be prepared by a vision to convert the Gentile Cornelius, so must Paul be summoned in a vision to go to Philippi to convert the Gentile Lydia. Luke seems to have known that Paul approved and supported female heads of house-churches, but she had not read Paul's Letter to the Philippians and so did not know that the female leaders of the church in Philippi were in fact named Euodia and Syntyche—the only women Paul mentions in this letter, written soon after his missionary visit to that city (see Phil. 4:2); it would seem that Paul had never heard of Lydia, who is Luke's fictional creation, invented to parallel Cornelius. But a great creation Lydia is, a typical powerful Lukan female, both a financially independent head of a household and a strong-willed, outspoken woman.

Just as Peter had to be pushed toward Cornelius, so Paul is the object of a determined divine nudging toward Lydia at Philippi. First Paul is "prevented by the Holy Spirit from delivering the message in the province of Asia," so he and his companions try to "enter Bithynia; but the Spirit of Jesus would not allow them": "During the night a vision came to Paul: a Macedonian stood there appealing to him and saying, 'Come across to Macedonia and help us.'" So Paul arrives under divine direction in the Macedonian city of Philippi:

> Here we stayed for some days, and on the Sabbath day we went outside the city gate by the river-side, where we thought there would be a place of prayer, and sat down and talked to the women who had gathered there. One of them named Lydia, a dealer in purple fabric from the city of Thyatira, who was a worshipper of God, was listening, and the Lord opened her heart to respond to what Paul said. She was baptized, and her household with her, and then she said to us, "If you have judged me to be a believer in the Lord,

Who Wrote The Gospels?

I beg you to come and stay in my house." And she insisted on our going. (Acts 16:13-15)

This is one of the most remarkable and mysterious passages in the New Testament. It stands at the beginning of the famous "we" passages in Acts, when Luke's narration suddenly shifts from third-person plural to first-person plural. No one has ever convincingly explained why Luke does so. The most immediately obvious explanation, that the author of Acts was a missionary companion of Paul, breaks down when we grasp the extent to which Paul was a legendary figure to Luke, not a personal intimate. But if one can speculate that Luke was a woman, an explanation comes forward. Remember that Luke insists in her gospel that Jesus' intimate circle included "many" women, though Luke, it would seem, knew the names of only three of them. And given Luke's habit of paralleled pairs, *so must Paul's*! Remember, too, that I argued earlier concerning the opening of the gospel of Luke that whenever Luke writes "we" or "us" about Christians she means to be gender-inclusive as well as ethnically-inclusive; if "both Jews and Gentiles" and "both men and women" are central to the meaning of Luke-Acts, then the "we" passages make sense. Luke would have known perfectly well that in the ancient world, both Jewish and Greco-Roman, what Paul is represented as doing at Philippi, publicly approaching and engaging in close dialogue with a respectable woman like Lydia, was simply unthinkable; Paul's action as described would mark Lydia as a prostitute: *unless Paul were accompanied by another woman.* "We" are present with Paul at Philippi, "we" who are both male and female, Jew and Gentile, and "we" make it possible for Paul to do what Luke describes, convert the Gentile woman Lydia, so that she becomes the first Gentile Christian on the European continent, even as the male Cornelius became the first Gentile Christian at Caesarea. The rest of the "we" passages in Acts fall into place as the consequence of this narrative necessity.

I do not mean to say that the author of Luke-Acts was an actual companion of Paul, only that Luke needs a female member of Paul's party at Philippi (who remains as nameless as the "many" women who accompanied Jesus on his journeys in Luke's Gospel), in order to construct her female-Gentile-convert parallel to the story of Cornelius.

V: Luke: Her Mind and Art

One more point: if the female leaders of the church at Philippi were really named Euodia and Syntyche (Phil. 4:2), why does Luke choose the name "Lydia"? That was the land of wealth, of the rich king Croesus. In the ancient world, "Lydian" was a by-word for riches: indeed, "*lydopathes*" meant "wealthy as a Lydian," and "*Lydia lithos*," "stone of Lydia," was a stone used to test gold. Throughout the Book of Acts, Luke stresses that it was "women of standing" who accepted the Christian message (Acts 13:50), "influential women" along with "godfearing Gentiles" who responded to Paul's preaching (Acts 17:4). Lydia, as a dealer in extremely expensive "purple fabric" (dyed with color extracted from murex and affordable only by the wealthy), was well-off, and head of a household (and thus widowed or unmarried like Martha in Luke's Gospel who invited Jesus into her home); for her entire "household with her" were baptized, following her lead (Acts 16:15). "Lydia" is thus the ideal name for the kind of women Luke describes as becoming Gentile Christians. Indeed, her home in Philippi became a house-church, the center of Christian activity in that city, for before Paul and his companions left Philippi, "on leaving the prison, they went to Lydia's house, where they met their fellow-Christians, and spoke words of encouragement to them; then they departed" (Acts 16:40). Luke deliberately parallels this scene to the earlier one, when Peter miraculously escaped from prison in Jerusalem: "When he realized how things stood, he made for the house of Mary, the mother of John Mark, where a large company was at prayer" (Acts 12:12).

In both scenes, the two apostles are delivered by miracle from prison, and in both, they go immediately to the house-church in the city (Jerusalem, Philippi) run by women (John Mark's mother; Lydia). Both houses are homes of well-to-do women (Mark's mother's is big enough for a "large company"; Lydia's is the home of a successful merchant with a sizable "household"). All this of course works as implicit presentation of Luke's theme that it was both Jewish "women of standing" and "influential" Gentile women who were leaders of house churches in earliest Christianity; but now comes the next most surprising literary fact about the Book of Acts: Peter's and Paul's miraculous escapes from prison are

Luke's borrowings from a scene in the *Bacchae* of Euripides.

All along in this book I have argued that authors of the New Testament read the Septuagint as a book about Jesus, as a collection of oracles understandable only in the light of the career of Jesus and (in Acts) of the early church. But it seems a bit much to say that Luke read Euripides as a prophet. If it can be shown that she did so, then we must enlarge our view of Luke's literary art.

Readers of both Luke and Euripides might already have had reason to suspect literary borrowing from *The Bacchae* in Luke's account of Paul's conversion in Acts 26. There a familiar sentence is added after "Saul, Saul, why do you persecute me?" The voice of the resurrected Jesus continues, "It is hard for you, this *kicking against the goads*" [*pros kentra laktizein*] (Acts 26:15). In *The Bacchae*, a persecuted god, Dionysus, cries out to his persecutor, Pentheus, that "you disregard my words of warning…and kick against the goads." Euripides' Greek in the last phrase is "*pros kentra lakti-zoimi*" (line 794); interestingly, Luke's term for "goads" is also in the plural [*kentra*]. Now one might object that Paul—or rather the risen Jesus!—is merely quoting a Greek proverb (though Paul has just declared that Jesus spoke to him in the "Jewish language" [Acts 26:14]), were it not that Luke borrows from this same play of Euripides in three other scenes in the Book of Acts. When Gamaliel warns the Jewish Council in Jerusalem that in continuing to persecute the Christians they risked finding themselves "at war with God" [*theomachoi*] (Acts 5:39), Luke uses what E. R. Dodds calls a "rather rare verb" that appears also in *The Bacchae* (line 45), an allusion that leads Dodds to suggest that Luke "had probably read the play" (Dodds, 1960, 68), especially when it is added to Luke's third striking allusion to Euripides' work in her scenes of Peter's and Paul's miraculous escapes from prison. When Peter is imprisoned in Jerusalem, an angel appears to him in the night, saying, "Quick! Get up." "And the chains fell away from his wrists." When they approach the iron gate of the prison, it "opened for them of its own accord" (Acts 12:8, 10). Likewise when Paul is imprisoned in Philippi, in the night there is an earthquake, and "all the doors burst open and all the prisoners found their fetters unfastened" (Acts 16:26). Such

V: Luke: Her Mind and Art

events are, says Dodds, "a traditional Dionysiac miracle" (1960, 132) and figure prominently in *The Bacchae* (lines 447-8), where the imprisoned followers of Dionysus find that "The chains on their legs snapped apart by themselves. Untouched by any human hand, the doors swung wide, opening of their own accord" (Grene and Lattimore, 1960, 560).

It really is not surprising that this play should have had such a lasting impact on Luke's imagination; for it concerns a young, persecuted and misunderstood deity, the son of Zeus and a mortal woman (Semele), who grants to his female followers redeeming release into religious ecstasy. Jesus, who was fathered by God on a woman as was Dionysus, grants the same to his followers. Male unbelievers in Dionysus imagine that the ecstasy is in fact drunkenness: "Religious ecstasy they call it. Dancing in honor of some new-fangled god, Some Dionysus—whoever he may be! They seem to need a couple of skins of wine for it too" (Curry, 1981, 126). Remember that in Jerusalem, too, unbelievers said of the Christians who were speaking in tongues of ecstasy, "They have been drinking" (Acts 2:13).

So Luke feels as free to create scenes on the basis of her reading (or having watched) a play of Euripides as she does to create scenes on the basis of her having read the Septuagint. Her amazing sense of freedom in this regard appears in yet another kind of composition; for just as Luke could read a passage in the Septuagint as predictive of events in the career of Jesus, she also saw events in the career of Jesus as predictive of events in the early history of Christianity. As the resurrection of the widow of Sarepta's son became the story of the widow of Nain, so Jesus' resurrection of Jairus' daughter became the pattern for Luke's story of Peter's resurrection of Dorcas. The name Jairus had been carefully chosen by Christian tradition as the name for the father of the child Jesus resurrects in the Gospel of Mark, for it is the Hebrew name *Yair*, "Let [God] arouse," and is thus expressive of the story's point while showing its paradigmatic and fictional nature. The Greek name *Dorkas* is equally significant to Luke: it means "gazelle," "so called from its large bright eyes" (Berry, 1958, 179), and is derived from *dedorka, derkomai*, "to look, see: hence to behold the light, or live" (Berry, 1958, 155). Luke would certainly have known the metaphorical meaning of Dorcas' name; and she also knew its Aramaic form, *Tabeitha*, "gazelle." But in its Aramaic form the name was significant to Luke because it is so close to what Jesus says to the dead daughter of Jairus in Mark: "Taleitha koum," literally, "Lamb, arise" (Mark 5:41). In Aramaic, while *tabeitha* means "gazelle," *Taleitha* means "lamb," or, metaphorically, "child." *Taleitha* gave Luke *Tabeitha* and thus *Dorkas*. Using this clue we can watch Luke basing her story of Peter's resurrecting Dorcas/Tabitha on Mark's story of Jesus' resurrecting the daughter of Jairus:

> In Joppa there was a disciple named Tabitha (in Greek, Dorcas, meaning a gazelle), who filled her days with acts of kindness and charity. At that time she fell ill and died; and they washed her body and laid it in a room upstairs. As Lydda was near Joppa, the disciples, who had heard that Peter was there, sent two men to him with the urgent request, "Please come over to us without delay." Peter thereupon went off with them. When he arrived they took him upstairs to the room, where all the widows came and stood round him in tears, showing him the shirts and coats that Dorcas used to make while she was with them. Peter sent them all outside, and knelt down and prayed. Then, turning towards the body, he said, "Get up, Tabitha." She opened her eyes, saw Peter, and sat up. He gave her his hand and helped her to her feet. (Acts 9:36-41)

In Mark's account, Jairus comes to Jesus and "pleads [*parakalei*]" with him, as in Acts, the Christians in Joppa sent an "urgent request [*parakalountes*]" about Dorcas. Since Jairus' daughter has "died [*apethanen*]," he wants Jesus to puts his "hands [*cheiras*]" on her, just as Dorcas' illness has caused her to "die [*apothanein*]," causing the need for Peter to give her his "hand [*cheira*]." When Jesus arrives at Jairus' house, he finds all "weeping [*klaiontas*]," as Peter, arriving in Joppa, finds Dorcas' friends "in tears [*klaiousai*]." Before performing his miracle, Jesus "put them all out [*ekbalon pantas*]," just as Peter "sent them all outside [*ekbalon...pantas*]." When Jesus says to the child, "Lamb [*Taleithe*] get up," she "stood up [*aneste*]," just as when Peter says to Dorcas, "Tabeitha, get up [*anastethi*]," he gives her his hand and "helped her to her feet [*anestesen*]." Luke concludes her story with a dramatic realization of Dorcas' name ("to behold the light, to live"): she "opened her eyes, and having seen Peter, sat up"

(Acts 9:40; parallels are in Mark 5:22-42).

If Peter resurrects a Jewish woman, Paul must, given Luke's habit of paralleling gender-pairs, resurrect a Gentile male. And as we might expect, his name will be as expressive of his fictional role as Dorcas' name was of hers; this time, the name is truly expressive—"Lucky" (*Eutychus*), and even seems to be part of a sly joke against Paul, who preaches such a long sermon at Troas that he starts putting people to sleep:

> Paul, who was to leave next day, addressed them, and went on speaking until midnight. Now there were many lamps in the upper room where we were assembled; and a youth named Eutychus, who was sitting on the window-ledge, grew more and more sleepy as Paul went on talking. At last he was completely overcome by sleep, fell from the third storey to the ground, and was picked up for dead. (Acts 20:7-9)

The lad is lucky that it was Paul who put him to sleep, for Paul proceeds to do for him just what Elisha did for the dead son of the woman of Shunem: the prophet "lay upon" the boy, grasped his hands, and "pressed upon him,)" whereupon the child "opened his eyes" (II Kings 4:34-35). Likewise Paul "threw himself upon him, seizing him in his arms," with the effect that the lucky "boy [was] led away alive" (Acts 20:10, 12).

The great freedom with which Luke writes of the career of Paul shows most famously in her fictional account of his vision on the road to Damascus that effected his conversion to Christianity. Luke starts her story with Paul, who has just approved of the stoning of the first Christian martyr, Stephen, going to the High Priest for "letters to the synagogues at Damascus authorizing him to arrest anyone he found, men or women, who followed the new way, and bring them to Jerusalem" (Acts 9:1-2). That the High Priest in Jerusalem did not in fact have the authority to arrest Jews in foreign states and extradite them to Palestine (Haenchen, 1971, 321) is our first clue that Luke's story is her own fiction. Haenchen points out that Luke here is probably speculating on the basis of her reading of I Maccabees 15, which says that the High Priest Simon had the authority (in the second century B.C.E.) to send envoys to Rome with letters; Rome in reply advised the arrest of any "traitors" against Israel: "hand them over to Simon the High Priest to be punished" (I Macc. 15:21; see Haenchen, 1971, 320). As it happens, the books of the Maccabees in the Septuagint control Luke's story to an even greater extent, for as Arthur Drews has written, "the whole account of Paul's conversion is modeled on that of Heliodorus, in II Macc. 3" (quoted in Haenchen, 1971, 326).

In his writings, Paul never described his conversion, an event about which he seemed quite reticent; the closest he ever comes is the simple statement in I Corinthians, "he appeared to me" (15:8). And we know that Luke had not read even this passage, for in 15:4, Paul writes that the risen Jesus appeared first to Peter, whereas Luke in her gospel gives us the post-Pauline story that Jesus appeared first on the road to Emmaus (a legend Paul did not know). In the absence of any account from Paul himself, Luke has brilliantly imagined the scene out of Septuagint Maccabees. There, Heliodorus, after consulting the High Priest, arrogantly enters the temple to remove its treasure. But Heliodorus (a name meaning "Gift of the Sun") instead finds himself in the presence of a "great apparition, so that all who presumed to come in with him, were astonished at the power of God, and fainted." Heliodorus himself "fell to the ground" [*pesonta pros tēn gēn*], and was "compasssed with great darkness" (II Macc.3:24, 27 LXX). Likewise Paul, after consulting the High Priest, went to arrest Christians, both men and women, but on the way a "light from the sky, more brilliant than the sun" [*heliou*—Luke is remembering Heliodorus] flashed about him. Paul then "fell upon the earth [*peson epi tēn gēn*]," as did all his companions, according to Luke's third version of this story, in Acts 26:14. Paul as a consequence is stricken blind, even as Heliodorus is "compassed with great darkness." Heliodorus is "carried out, being unable to help himself" (II Macc. 3:28), just as Paul has to be "led by the hand" (Acts 9:8) after his blinding experience. Later, Onias the High Priest is asked to intercede to save Heliodorus' life, as Ananias of Damascus is asked to intercede to save Paul's vision (II Macc. 3:31; Acts 9:10).

This final appearance of the resurrected Jesus in Luke-Acts, to the extent that it is based on Luke's memory of the Books of Maccabees, brings us full circle back to his first appearance at the end of Luke's gospel,

V: Luke: Her Mind and Art

for Luke's supplementing of Mark to supply a Resurrection appearance at the empty tomb may also have been influenced by II Maccabees. Part of the apparition to Heliodorus involved "two young men of surpassing strength and glorious beauty, splendidly dressed. They stood on either side of him," and he "fell to the ground" (II Macc. 3:26-27). Likewise at the empty tomb the women find that "all of a sudden two men in dazzling garments were at their side." The women were "terrified," and turned their faces to the earth, just as Heliodorus and his men were "faint with terror, stricken with panic" at the apparition, and "fell suddenly to the ground" (Luke 24:4; II Macc. 3:24,26).

The addition of a Resurrection appearance is not, of course, the only change Luke makes in Mark's final chapter. Mark had allowed the three women at the empty tomb the terror of hearing "He has been raised again," but not the joy of proclaiming it: "They said nothing to anybody, for they were afraid" (Mark 16:6,8). It would seem that in Mark's view, mere women could only respond to the angel's announcement by silently "trembling with amazement" (16:8). In contrast, Luke's Mary responds with an almost impertinent pluckiness to another angelic annunciation: "How can this be? I am still a virgin" (Luke 1:34). Mark seems to have believed that women were just not up to the strain of dealing with the shock of an unexpectedly empty tomb and the command to "go and give this message to his disciples" (Mark 16:7). Though Mark had surely not reached the level of misogyny evinced by Peter in the gnostic gospel of Thomas ("Let Mary leave us, for women are not worthy of life" [Thomas 114]), it is nonetheless clear that Mark held proclamation of the Resurrection faith to be men's work. Indeed the gospel of Mark gives us the first post-Pauline evidence of what Clarice J. Martin calls the "process of the patriarchalization of the earliest church" (Schüssler Fiorenza, 1994, 772).

In this regard, Luke was rather closer to the Gnostics than to the growing misogyny of the orthodox tradition; for Luke changes Mark's ending: "returning from the tomb, they reported all this to the Eleven and all the others" (Luke 24:9). Just as Luke uses Peter's great speech at Pentecost to state her central theme "both men and women," the Gnostics, using a reverse tactic, employed Peter as the spokesman for a misguided anti-feminism. In the Gnostic Gospel of Mary, for example, Peter becomes outraged on learning that the resurrected Jesus had appeared to Mary Magdalene:

> "Did he really speak with a woman without our knowledge (and) not openly? Are we to turn about and listen to her? Did he prefer her to us?" Then Mary wept and said to Peter, "My brother Peter, what do you think? Do you think that I thought this up myself in my heart, or that I am lying about the Savior?" Levi answered and said to Peter, "Peter, you have always been hot-tempered. Now I see you contending against the woman like the adversaries. But if the Savior made her worthy, who are you indeed to reject her?" (Robinson, 1988, 526-527)

As Levi grasps, Peter speaks like "the adversaries," that is, orthodox Christians, who were already by the end of the first century establishing the kind of patriarchal domination of the church that Luke and the Gnostics were fighting against. So Luke changes Mark's final words—as she changes so much else in her sources—to align with one of her greatest themes, "both men and women."

"Lost Gospels": Thomas and Q

B<small>Y NOW IT IS OBVIOUS</small> that the answer to who wrote the gospels? is far more complicated than the simply Matthew, Mark, Luke, and John. To complicate the story even more, we need to take seriously the implications of Luke's remark that before her time (around 100 C.E.) "many writers" had "undertaken to draw up an account" of Christian origins (Luke 1:1). By the end of the first century, there weren't *four* gospels, there were *many*, and a scholarly consensus is forming that with regard to those many gospels not found in the Bible, "the epithets 'heretical' and 'orthodox' are meaningless," Helmut Koester argues in his preface: "only dogmatic prejudice can assert that the canonical writings have an exclusive claim to apostolic origin and thus to historical priority" (Koester, 1990, xxx). Koester knows that his idea is a "new orientation" in gospel studies, one that has brought the "apocryphal writings...into the center of the scholarly debate" (1990, xxx-xxxi).

Scholars like Helmut Koester realize that informed biblical study must deal not only with the Gospels of Matthew, Mark, Luke and John, but also with such works as the Gospels of Thomas and Peter, the "Q Gospel," the "Signs Gospel," and the Secret Gospel of Mark. As Arthur Dewey argues, the non- canonical gospels "must be reevaluated," since "New Testament scholarship has long since undermined" the old idea that the canonical four Gospels have exclusive claim to an "earlier, historical kernel" while works like the Gospel of Peter were merely "dependent" on Matthew, Mark, Luke and John (Miller, 1992, 393-4). Dewey insists, on the contrary, that all those "many" gospels, including the canonical four, are "witnesses to a very complex interpretive enterprise,...were subject to the various formats and patterns of ancient communication, [and] cannot be simple historical reports" (Miller, 1992, 394). So it is not simply that we find only "history" in the canonical four and "fiction" or "legend" in the rest; rather we have a large body of early Christian literature, some in the Bible and some not, and all of it must be taken into account if we wish to understand early Christianity. The author of the Gospel of Thomas was a Christian, as were the authors of Q and the Gospel of Peter; it is not for us to decide that they were any "less Christian" than, say, the author of Matthew. Studying "lost" gospels will help confirm that the canonical four were not the last word about Jesus— and certainly not the first—and that the four are no less likely to contain theological fictions than the "many" that Luke mentioned.

Some think complacently, and wrongly, that while contemporary Christianity may lack doctrinal unity, the early church was at one; but in fact the reverse is true: there is more Christian theological unity in the twentieth century than there was in the first two. Most Christians today could recite without much apparent qualm the Apostles' Creed, but that was not the case nineteen hundred years ago, when several profoundly different understandings of Jesus were competing for primacy. As the author of the First Letter of John argued, some in his area who regarded themselves as Christians were in fact "antichrists," since they did not believe that "Jesus Christ came in the flesh" (I John 4:2). Or as Paul wrote to the Christians at Corinth, while some there call themselves "Paul's," some are for "Apollos," some "follow Cephas," only some others are "Christ's" (I Cor. 1:12). Paul knew about four different sects at Corinth already in the fifties—in just one city!

Among the many sects of first-century Christians, this chapter will concern the first of two broad and conflicting parties: (1) those who saw Jesus as a teacher of wisdom who came to tell us how to live or how to know our true nature, and (2) those who saw Jesus as a dying and reviving god crucified for our sins who rose again as guarantor of our own resurrection on the last day. The first is found in such works as Q and the Gospel of Thomas, the second in the theology of Paul (as in I Cor. 15). The four canonical Gospels reveal major struggles to combine the two.

In the final chapters of this book I present an argument that there are, embedded within the Fourth Gospel, *two* "lost gospels"—the hypothetical work now called the "Signs Gospel" plus another much-enlarged version thereof, one that was in turn revised by a third author to become what we now call the Gospel of John. In this chapter I argue that we might better understand such strenuous literary activity by seeing it in the context of something analogous, the story of two other "lost gospels," the Gospel of Thomas and the hypothetical Synoptic Sayings Source, generally called "Q."

The concept of "lost gospels" has received widespread attention in recent years through publication of such books as James Robinson's edition of *The Nag Hammadi Library* (a collection of early Christian and other texts containing the only known copy of the Gospel of Thomas), and Burton Mack's *The Lost Gospel: The Book of* Q *and Christian Origins.* Thomas and Q are the main focus of this chapter, partially as preface to the next three, as I try to point out how some very similar material in these two lost Gospels could yet serve as basis for two totally opposing trajectories in early Christian thought, the one gnostic and anti-apocalyptic (Thomas), the other apocalyptic and eschatological (Q).

Gospels became "lost" in the ancient world when people stopped making copies of them, and rare manuscripts crumbled or were destroyed. Books and scrolls were precious few as it was, since every one had to be laboriously hand-copied, letter by letter; and the fact, for example, that not a single copy of the Gospel of Mark survives from the first two centuries, and only one from the third (Manuscript P45), shows how very close even so important a work as this gospel could come to being lost through lack of a felt need to make multiple copies of it. Now Mark nearly became lost because that was what Matthew and Luke *intended* should become of it; once they had, independently of each other, produced revised and expanded versions of Mark by combining it with Q and other material, they certainly did not expect or desire that some day their books would flank Mark, cheek by jowl, in a larger work we now call the New Testament. Rather, they both expected that their work would render Mark superfluous, and that Mark would simply wither away—as very nearly happened.

That what nearly happened to the Gospel of Mark did indeed happen to the other major written source for the authors of Matthew and Luke—the hypothetical Gospel "Q"—is the contention of what is now the great majority of New Testament scholars (Koester, 1990, 129); Q is now accepted as what Burton Mack calls a "lost gospel." It may be said that the re- discovery of that other great lost Gospel, Thomas, provided the final blow to conservative opposition to the idea that Q once existed as an actual Christian document. Since hypothetical Q is said to be a work consisting almost entirely of sayings of Jesus, with no narrative context, no "gospel story" at all, and since no other such early Christian "sayings gospel" was known to exist, it was not difficult for some to argue that Q exists only in the minds of critical scholars. But then the Gospel of Thomas was discovered in Egypt in 1945, and by the 1970s was widely published, translated into various modern languages from its Coptic text: and Thomas is exactly what Q was said to be, a collection of sayings of Jesus with no narrative context, no "gospel story," at all. The Gospel of Thomas proves that some early Christians wrote works consisting only of sayings; Q is now accepted as being one of them, though no copy of it has ever been found and it is only knowable as it can be extracted from the Gospels of Matthew and Luke. Even though the theologies of Thomas and Q are very different from each other, surprisingly large parts of both works stem from the same body of very early Jesus-sayings material, for many of the sayings in Thomas are nearly identical to those in Q. How such similar sayings in these two lost gospels could serve as bases for two very different understandings of Jesus will be the point of the rest of this chapter and will serve as introduction to my argument in the final part of this book.

Of the 114 sayings attributed to Jesus in the Gospel of Thomas, 44 have close parallels in Q, while five have parallels in the Gospel of John. I append a list of the parallels at the end of this chapter. Though only five Thomas sayings have parallels in John, Thomas is closer in spirit, in theology, to John than to Q, so that Thomas and John both became gospels beloved by gnostic Christians in the second century, while Q served as a text about Jesus for some early eschatological, apocalyptic Christians who expected the imminent return of Jesus as Son of Man. And while the

VII: "Lost Gospels": Thomas and Q

theologies of Thomas and Q are quite different, both gospels belong to the same genre, one closely related to the Wisdom tradition in Judaism that produced such biblical books as Proverbs and Ecclesiastes; both Thomas and Q are collections of the "sayings of the wise" teacher, Jesus of Nazareth (to use the formula of Prov. 1:6). I begin with Thomas.

The Gospel of Thomas is now generally taken to be the work of an early Christian group, "most likely in Syria" (Robinson, 1988, 14), that was in the process of "taking its first steps in the direction of Gnosticism" (Miller, 1992, 34). The story of the discovery of the Gospel of Thomas in an ancient Coptic-language collection of Gnostic texts near Nag Hammadi in Egypt in 1945 has become justly famous. In December of that year, an Egyptian peasant named Muhammad Ali, digging for nitrates near the foot of Jabal al Tarif, discovered a large sealed clay pot partially buried. Hoping for treasure and overcoming his fear that the jar contained an evil *jinn*, he broke it with his mattock, only to find instead twelve leather-bound volumes plus leaves of a thirteenth, containing in all some fifty-two separate religious and philosophical tractates from the early centuries C.E.—along with the Dead Sea Scrolls the most important discoveries of ancient religious texts in our time. James M. Robinson tells this story in his edition of *The Nag Hammadi Library* (1988, 22-23), which contains the English translations of the Coptic-language Gnostic texts used in this chapter.

Christian Gnostics were called such because they claimed to possess the saving knowledge (*gnōsis* in Greek) that was revealed to them (or to such original Christians as John, James, Thomas or Mary Magdalene) by Jesus himself. This secret knowledge alone granted salvation, since the Gnostics maintained that the orthodox tradition had totally failed to understand Jesus. According to the Apocalypse of Peter, the "men of the propagation of falsehood," are those who "cleave to the name of a dead man," the Jesus of the flesh. The real "living Savior" is an "incorporeal body"; "But this one into whose hands and feet they drive the nails is his fleshly part, which is the substitute being put to shame, the one who came into being in his likeness" (Robinson 374, 377). With texts such as this, we can now learn what the Gnostics "knew."

First of all, they knew that the Creator in the Hebrew Bible was not really God, but was in fact a "malicious grudger" who "refused Adam from eating the tree of knowledge." "What kind of god is this?" (Robinson, 1988, 455). At the hands of this incompetent non-god, "The world came about through a mistake. For he who created it wanted to create it imperishable and immortal. He fell short of attaining his desire. For the world never was imperishable, nor, for that matter, was he who made the world" (Gospel of Philip; Robinson, 1988, 154). A major part of that "mistake" was the separation into two beings of the original androgynous human: "When Eve was still in Adam death did not exist. When she was separated from him death came into being. If he enters again and attains his former self, death will be no more" (Gospel of Philip; Robinson, 1988, 150). Re-attaining that original and immortal unity by transcending sexuality was the goal of at least some Christian Gnostics:

> Jesus said to them, "When you make the two one, and when you make the inside like the outside and the outside like the inside and the above like the below, and when you make the male and the female one and the same, so that the male not be male nor the female female...then you will enter [the kingdom]." (Gospel of Thomas; Robinson, 1988, 129)

Attainment of this immortal union requires self-knowledge of one's own divine sonship: "Nothing will be able to receive imperishability if it does not first become a son" (Gospel of Philip; Robinson, 1988, 154). "Sonship" is the original pre-sexual androgyny of Adam, attainable again only by the Gnostic: "the kingdom is inside of you, and it is outside of you. When you come to know yourselves, then you will become known, and you will realize that it is you who are the sons of the living father" (Gospel of Thomas; Robinson, 1988, 126). Indeed, "When you make the two one, you will become the sons of man" (Gospel of Thomas; Robinson, 1988, 137). For the Gnostic, salvation means coming to recognize one's own inner divine nature, one's own sonship that was lost in Adam's "separation": "Because of this, Christ came to repair the separation which was from the beginning and again unite the two, and to give life to those who

VII: "Lost Gospels": Thomas and Q

died as a result of the separation and unite them" (Gospel of Philip; Robinson, 1988, 151).

Gnostic "knowing" is self-knowledge of one's own true inner divine nature: "When you come to know yourselves" you will enter the kingdom, or return to the pre-material, predivided state. Of course "knowing" of such primal unity requires a radical asceticism, an ending of all sexuality; this may well be a chief reason why Christian Gnosticism lost out in the early sectarian competition. As the Gnostic Testimony of Truth has it, since "Christ passed through a virgin's womb," "let us therefore strengthen [ourselves] as virgins" (Robinson, 1988, 452-453). Indeed, the author of this Gnostic text allegorized Jesus' encounter with John the Baptist as an overcoming of the sexual urge: "John bore witness to the [descent] of Jesus. For it is he who saw the [power] which came down upon the Jordan river; for he knew that the dominion of carnal procreation had come to an end. The Jordan river is the power of the body, that is, the senses of pleasures. The water of the Jordan is the desire for sexual intercourse" (Robinson, 1988, 450).

Like other Gnostic Christian texts, the Testimony of Truth has no more interest in literal water baptism than it has in bodily resurrection at the last day; for "carnal resurrection is destruction" (Robinson 451): "For [the Son] of Man did not baptize any of his disciples. But [if] these who were baptized were headed for life, the world would become empty. And the fathers of baptism were defiled. But the baptism of truth is something else; it is by renunciation of [the] world that it is found" (Robinson, 1988, 457). The Gnostic renouncer already has it all: "He who has been anointed possesses everything. He possesses the resurrection, the light, the cross, the holy spirit...This is the kingdom of heaven" (Gospel of Philip; Robinson, 1988, 153-154).

This is one of the most striking of Gnostic Christian teachings, that the true "knower" *already has* eternal life: "already you have the resurrection," declares the Gnostic Treatise on the Resurrection (Robinson, 1988, 56), for "The Savior swallowed up death": "We suffered with him, and we arose with him, and we went to heaven with him" (Robinson, 1988, 54-55).

Here, of course, readers of the Gospel of John (a favorite of second-century Gnostics) will be strongly reminded of such passages as the ones saying that the believer "has already passed from death to life," "The believer possesses eternal life," and "This is eternal life, to know [*ginōskōsi*] thee" (John 5:24; 6:48; 17:3).

The orthodox tradition tried hard to eliminate such beliefs (even going so far as to re-write a nearly Gnostic version of the Gospel of John, as we shall see), and condemned some Gnostic teachers by name: "the infection of their teaching will spread like a gangrene. Such are Hymenaeus and Philetus; they have shot wide of the truth in saying that our resurrection has already taken place, and are upsetting people's faith" (II Tim. 2:17-18).

Of course one of the effects of this Gnostic doctrine that the believer already "possesses the resurrection" is that texts like the Gospel of Thomas are profoundly anti-apocalyptic; the kingdom of God is not some future hope but a present reality:

> His disciples said to him, "When will the kingdom come?" [Jesus said,] "It will not come by waiting for it. It will not be a matter of saying, 'here it is' or 'there it is.' Rather, the kingdom of God is spread out upon the earth, and men do not see it." (Robinson, 1988, 138)

And only some few—the "knowers"—will be able to have this insight: "Whoever finds the interpretation of these sayings will not experience death" (Gospel of Thomas; Robinson, 1988, 126). They alone understand that "the kingdom is inside of you, and it is outside of you. When you come to know yourselves, then you will become known, and you will realize that you are sons of the living father" (Robinson, 1988, 126). Verses like this last show how far the Christian community that produced the Gospel of Thomas had moved toward the Gnostic idea that knowledge of one's true divine nature is the essence of Christianity. For in Thomas, eschatology becomes deeply personal:

> The disciples said to Jesus, "Tell us how our end will be." Jesus said, "Have you discovered, then, the beginning, that you look for the end? For where the beginning is, there will the end be. Blessed is he who will take his place in the beginning; he will know the end and will not experience death." (Robinson 128)

Those who come to know their own divine nature are already *in* the kingdom:

> His disciples said to him, "When will the repose of the dead come about, and when will the new world come?" He said to them, "What you look forward to has already come, but you do not recognize it." (Robinson 132)

In the sort of first-century apocalyptic Christianity that produced the Book of Revelation, "repose" comes only to martyrs who "die in the faith"; it is they who will "rest from their labors" (Rev. 14:13). For Thomas Christians, on the other hand, "repose" meant "to find one's place again in unity with the highest God" (Funk 502), rather than in some future time. This aspect of Thomas—that the kingdom "has already come"—is strikingly similar to a theme in the Gospel of John, one that has come to be called "realized eschatology" (as opposed to the "future eschatology" that runs through most of the New Testament). In the Fourth Gospel, Jesus declares that "the time is coming, indeed it is already here, when the dead shall hear the voice of the Son of God, and those who hear shall come to life" (John 5:25). There is a sense in the Gospel of John, as in Thomas, that eternal life is now, not in the future, for "whoever heeds what I say and puts his trust in him who sent me has eternal life; he does not come up to judgment, but has already passed from death to life" (John 5:24).

This is part of what I meant when I said above that Thomas is closer in spirit to the Fourth Gospel than to Q; for both John and Thomas turn "life" and "death" into metaphors, into spiritual matters of knowing and not knowing. For just as John has Jesus declare that "This is eternal life: to know you the only true God, and Jesus Christ whom you have sent" (John 17:3), so Thomas has Jesus declare of his words that "Whoever knows them will not taste death" (Thomas 19). There will be much more about "realized eschatology" in the Fourth Gospel in the chapters below; in the meantime, the differences between Thomas and Q await us.

As I said above, some 44 sayings in Thomas have parallels in Q. Both works stem from early collections of sayings attributed to Jesus, but they have already begun to diverge significantly in their understandings of Jesus and his teachings. Burton Mack has aptly described the differences between Thomas and Q with regard to apocalypticism and the "son of man" described in Daniel 7, calling the "Gospel of Thomas a proto-gnostic treatise…From the options available in Q and Mark, the Thomas people rejected the mythology of the apocalyptic son of Man" (1993, 183). The Christians who produced the Gospel of Thomas were aware of the designation of Jesus as the Son of Man, but had no interest in the apocalyptic uses of the term; nor did they look for Jesus to return on the clouds, as did other Christians who applied Daniel 7:14 to their hope of Jesus' Second Coming. Instead, Thomas Christians insisted that "Jesus said, 'When you make the two one, you will become the sons of man'" (Thomas 106). Any Christian can become a "son of man," for "Jesus said, 'He who will drink from my mouth will become like me. I myself shall become he'" (Thomas 108).

How two early Christian groups can take the same traditional saying of Jesus and move it both into apocalyptic and non-apocalyptic directions shows clearly in Thomas 20 and Q/Luke 13:18-19:

> The disciples said to Jesus, "Tell us what the kingdom of heaven is like." He said to them;, "It is like a mustard seed. It is the smallest of all seeds. But when it falls on tilled soil, it produces a great plant and becomes a shelter for birds of the sky." (Thomas 20) "What is the kingdom of God like?" he continued. "What shall I compare it with? It is like a mustard-seed which a man took and sowed in his garden; and it grew to be a tree [*dendron*] and the birds of heaven [*ouranou*] came to roost [*kateskēnosen*] among its branches [*kladois*] (Q/Luke 13:18-19; here I follow the scholarly convention of quoting Q passages from Luke not Matthew).

The Q version of this saying has been accommodated to an apocalyptic passage in the Book of Daniel, where Nebuchadnezzar's dream is interpreted by Daniel to show that the "Most High" gives the "kingdom to whom he will" (Dan. 4:32). In that dream a tree (*dendron*) of great height appeared, in which animals "took shelter" (*kateskēnoun*), and birds of "heaven" (*ouranou*) roosted in its branches (*kladois*) (Dan. 4:8-9 LXX). Apocalyptically-minded Christians rephrased the saying, re-interpreting it with vocabulary from the Greek version of the Book of Daniel, whereas the non-apocalyptic Thomas community had no interest in injecting Daniel's apocalypticism into sayings of Jesus.

Recognizing this tension between apocalyptic and anti-apocalyptic understandings of Jesus will be a key to the complex history of the Gospel of John, as we shall see in the remainder of this book.

Q/Thomas Parallels

Q/LUKE	THOMAS	KEY PHRASE
Q 6:20	54	Blessed are poor
Q 6:21	69	Blessed are hungry
Q 6:22	68	Blessed when hated
Q 6:31	6	Golden Rule
Q 6:34	95	Not lend at interest
Q 6:39	34	Blind leading blind
Q 6:41-2	26	Speck in eye
Q 6:43	43	Good tree, bad fruit
Q 6:44-5	45	Figs from thorns
Q 7:24-5	78	A reed swaying?
Q 7:28	46	Greater than John
Q9:58	86	Foxes have holes
Q 10:2	72	Harvest is great
Q 10:8-9	14	Eat what is given
Q 10:22	61	Everything from my Father
Q 10:23-4	17	Eye has not seen
Q 11:9-10	92, 94	Seek and find

Q/Thomas Parallels (continued)

Q 11:27-8	79	Blessed the womb
Q 11:33	33	Lamp under bushel
Q 11:34-5	24	Lamp of the body
Q 11:39-40	89	Wash outside of cup
Q 11:52	39	Keys of knowledge
Q 12:2 5,	6	Nothing hidden
Q 12:3	33	Shouted from housetops
Q 12:10	44	Blaspheme spirit
Q 12:13-14	73	Divide possessions
Q 12:16-21	63	The rich fool
Q 12:22-31	36	Consider the lilies
Q 12:33	76	Treasure in heaven
Q 12:39	21, 13	Thief in the night
Q 12:49	10	Fire on the earth
Q 12:51-3	16	Peace on earth
Q 12:56	91	When you see clouds
Q 13:18-19	20	Mustard seed
Q 13:20-21	96	Kingdom like yeast
Q 14:16-24	6	A banquet
Q 14:26	55, 101	Hate father, mother
Q 14:27	55	Take up cross
Q 15:3-7	17	Lost sheep
Q 16:13	47	Serve two masters
Q 17:6	48	Tree into sea
Q 17:20-21	113	Kingdom among you
Q 17:34	61	Two in a bed
Q 19:26	41	Who has will be given more

(Adapted from Koester 88-89)

Thomas/John Parallels

THOMAS	JOHN	KEY PHRASE
1	8:51-2	Not taste death
24	8:12; 9:5	Light of the world
31	4:44	No prophet honored
38	7:34,36	Seek me but not find me
71	2:19	Destroy this temple

❧ VII ❧

Who Wrote the Gospel of John, and How Did They Do It?

As this story unfolds we begin to see a pattern: Matthew and Luke were revised and expanded versions of an earlier and by-then outdated Gospel of Mark, to which they added, among other things, sayings of Jesus (from Q) and resurrection appearances (from sources M and L). Similarly, the Gospel of John is a revised and expanded version of an earlier gospel, to which John has added, among other things, sayings of Jesus and resurrection appearances. Only this time, the matter is much more difficult to deal with, because John did not go to Mark and Q, as did Matthew and Luke, but to another source, and that source no longer exists.

It is fairly easy to work out how Matthew and Luke recast Mark, because we have all three of these gospels to cross-check; and it is even relatively easy to reconstruct the hypothetical document Q, because we have both Matthew's and Luke's independent quotations of it: recent efforts to do so are readily available from John Kloppenborg (1987), Burton Mack (1993), and Arland Jacobson (1992). This is not the case with the Gospel of John, because there is no parallel user of John's source for us to cross-check. Q became what Burton Mack calls a "lost gospel" because it was superfluous after Matthew and Luke had reproduced so much of it in their works. Mark *almost* became a lost gospel in the same way, for it very nearly disappeared from the manuscript tradition: there are no copies or fragments of Mark from the first or second century, and only one from the third, while there are eight of Matthew and four of Luke from the second and third centuries (Koester, 1990, 314, 332).

John's main source likewise became a lost gospel; we no longer have it and can only reconstruct it by extracting it from between the seams where it is embedded in the Fourth Gospel. Again, this has recently, and brilliantly, been done by Robert Fortna, in *The Fourth Gospel and its Predecessor* (1988). I plan respectfully to build on this work in what follows.

John had open in front of him as he composed his gospel a written source, one in some ways strikingly parallel to the Gospel of Mark. A consensus title has formed for this hypothetical work and I shall adopt it here: "The Signs Gospel" (Miller, 1992, 175). As Fortna has recently written in *The Complete Gospels*:

> The Signs Gospel is reconstructed chiefly by looking for points in John where obvious literary seams appear; such seams often indicate inconsistencies and even contradictions in the text of the completed gospel. These rough spots are infrequent in the synoptic gospels, even where Matthew or Luke reproduces material from Mark or Q. But they are common in John and seem to suggest that when using the hypothetical "source" the author of John quoted it practically verbatim; the author simply allowed the rough connections and inconsistencies to stand. (in Miller, 1992, 175)

The complexities do not end here. The author whom we call "John" and who wrote with a copy of the Signs Gospel open in front of him did not have the last word. Another author treated the first edition of John's Gospel in something like the same way John treated the Signs Gospel (and as Matthew and Luke treated Mark)—revising and expanding it into its present form. I shall call the reviser of the Signs Gospel "John," and the reviser of John I shall call "John 2." There were striking theological and ecclesiastical differences between them, as we shall see, and a clear understanding of the complexities of the Fourth Gospel requires unraveling of these different layers.

That complex layering is clear at the end of the next-to-last chapter of John, which despite its placement twenty-five verses from the end looks exactly like a conclusion: "There were indeed many other signs that Jesus performed in the presence of his disciples, which are not recorded in this book. Those here written have been recorded in order that you may hold the faith that Jesus is the Christ, the Son of God, and that through this faith you may possess life by his name" (John 20:30-31).

VII: *Who Wrote the Gospel of John, and How Did They Do It?*

Despite the concluding tone of these words, we find yet another chapter, which then concludes with a formula that looks very much like an imitation of the earlier ending, though without any interest in a notion of "signs": "There is much else that Jesus did. If it were all to be recorded in detail, I suppose the whole world could not hold the books that would be written" (John 21:25).

Helmut Koester speaks for a scholarly consensus when he writes that "John 21, though belonging to the older stages of the transmission of the text, is certainly a later appendix" (1990, 246). Ernst Haenchen also expresses what is coming to be a consensus view:

> We must reckon with three different authors: (a) the author of the "gospel of miracles," which understands the "signs" (*sēmeia*) as miracles certifying faith; (b) an "evangelist" who interprets the "signs" (*sēmeia*) as pointers, through Jesus Christ, to the revelation of the invisible God, "the Father of Jesus Christ," pointers whose meaning becomes visible for the first time only through the gift of the spirit at Easter; and (c) an ecclesiastical "supplementer," or redactor, who appends the proclamation of the imminent end of the world, of the sacraments, and of an ethic that conceives of Christians as the elite among good men. (Haenchen, 1984, 39)

There is a long history among these three works, as the first and third of them are perhaps fifty years apart.

Let us start with the author of the Signs Gospel. He was a Greek-speaking Jewish Christian of the mid-first century, who was deeply familiar with the Greek Septuagint version of the Hebrew Bible, and who regarded Jesus as a new or antitypical Moses. We know this because of the importance he attaches to the Greek word *sēmeia*, "signs." Jesus' miracles are "signs" that cause belief in him, an idea borrowed from the Septuagint account of Moses' miracles: Moses "performed the signs [*epoiēse ta sēmeia*] before the people. And the people believed [*episteusen*]" (Ex. 4:30-31 LXX). Likewise at Cana in Galilee, Jesus "performed the first of the signs [*epoiēsen archēn tōn sēmeiōn*], and his disciples believed [*episteusan*]" (John 2:11). According to the author of the Signs Gospel, the "signs Jesus performed [*sēmeia epoiēsen ho Iēsous*]" were written down in order that readers "may believe [*pisteuēte*] that Jesus is the Christ" (John 20:30, 31). The exact accordance with Septuagint vocabulary is no accident: a new Moses is here, in the view of the Signs author, the very one Moses himself had predicted: "The LORD said to me,...'I will raise up for them a prophet like you, one of their own race, and I will put my words into his mouth'" (Deut. 18:18). In order to demonstrate that Jesus is indeed the new prophet, the promised Messiah, the Signs Gospel presents, according to Fortna, seven miracle stories as "signs" intended to cause faith in Jesus as Messiah: Jesus changes water into wine (now preserved in John 2:1-11); Jesus heals an official's son at a distance (now in John 4:46-54); Jesus provides a huge catch of fish (now in John 21:1-14); Jesus feeds five thousand, and then walks on the Sea of Galilee (now in John 6:1-25); Jesus raises Lazarus from the dead (now in John 11:1-45); Jesus gives sight to a blind man (now in John 9:1-18); and Jesus heals a crippled man (now in John 5:2-9). Three of the seven (the first three in the list above) are numbered by the Signs author in his account, so there is some reason to believe that in the original Signs Gospel all seven (an important symbolic number in biblical numerology implying perfection or completeness) were given numbers. Strikingly, three of these "signs" closely parallel miracle stories in the Synoptic Gospels: healing at a distance (as in Luke 7 and Matthew 8), the huge catch of fish (as in Luke 5), and the feeding of the five thousand (as in Mark 6 and parallels in Matt. 14 and Luke 9). But since there are no close *verbal* parallels between John and the Synoptics in these stories—no examples of the same words in the same order—we can conclude that the Signs author was not using the Synoptics as a source, or vice versa—indeed the Signs Gospel probably pre-dated all three Synoptics—but rather that the Signs author went to the same kinds of oral tradition about Jesus that writers such as Mark did. And this tells us something very important about the Signs author: he was, like other gospel writers, at the third (or greater) remove from the historical Jesus and was not an eyewitness. So even though, as we shall see later, "John 2" believed that "John" was an eyewitness to the Crucifixion and resurrection (John 19:26; 21:24), this cannot be the case, since "John" was dependent upon an

VII: *Who Wrote the Gospel of John, and How Did They Do It?*

earlier written source—the Signs Gospel—whose author was not an eye-witness either.

Fortna argues that the Signs author was a *Jewish* Christian, part of a "Greek-speaking Jewish synagogue" whose members "believed that Jesus was the Messiah. The religion of these believers was Judaism. They were 'Christian' only in the literal sense,…believers in Jesus as the Christ" (in Miller, 1992, 176). These Jewish Christians had collected traditions about Jesus that they hoped would prove he was the Messiah. They lived in a cosmopolitan atmosphere, in a Greek-speaking city (Alexandria, I shall argue later), for some of their traditions about Jesus have an ultimately pagan origin: water changed into wine (borrowed from Dionysus mythology) and Lazarus resurrected (borrowed from Osiris mythology). Other traditions in the Signs Gospel are recastings of stories in the Septuagint, read as a book about Jesus. For the Signs author regarded Jesus not only as the new Moses, but also as the "prophet we await," foreshadowed by Elijah and Elisha. This is why the Fourth Gospel has John the Baptist deny not only that he is the "Messiah," but also that he is either "the prophet" or "Elijah" (John 1:21); for these roles—Messiah, prophet, Elijah—belong to Jesus. Although the Synoptic Gospels present John the Baptist as Elijah (as in Matt. 17:12-13), the Fourth Gospel presents *Jesus* as the one fulfilling Malachi 4:5: "I will send you the prophet Elijah before the great and terrible day of the LORD comes." One way it does so is by re-writing stories about Elijah and his successor Elisha as typological stories about Jesus; a clear example is the story of the feeding of the five thousand. This account in the Signs Gospel finds its origin in the Septuagint story of Elisha's feeding a hundred men with twenty loaves of bread. In that account, Elisha's servant, or boy (*paidarion*) is told to serve a hundred men with twenty barley loaves (*artous krithinous*). The Signs Gospel repeats the details: a "boy" (*paidarion*) has five barley loaves (*artous krithinous*). Both prophets instruct their disciples to feed the people with the inadequate amount of bread, and in both cases the disciples protest with rhetorical questions: "Why should I set these before a hundred men?" (IV Kings 4:43 LXX); "What is that among so many?" (John 6: 9). In both cases the seemingly insufficient food supplies the large crowd, the difference being that Jesus' miracle is stupendously greater: five thousand fed with five loaves as compared to one hundred fed with twenty (though in both cases the loaves multiply by a factor of five). And whereas in Elisha's case the men only "ate," in Jesus' miracle the five thousand took "as much as they wanted," and were "filled" (John 6:11-12).

This is one of the very few miracles the Fourth Gospel shares with the three Synoptics: Jesus also feeds five thousand with five loaves in Mark 6 (parallels in Matt. 14 and Luke 9). But there is no direct literary relationship between Mark and the Signs Gospel here; both draw upon Christian tradition based on the Books of Kings. But whereas the Signs Gospel uses the vocabulary of the Septuagint, Mark does not, appearing rather to draw upon a tradition based on Aramaic readings of Kings. We know this from differences in vocabulary: though Elisha in the Septuagint tells his disciple to "Give to the people and let them eat" [*dote tō laō kai esthietōsan*] (IV Kings 4:42 LXX), Mark's Jesus says "Give to them...to eat" [*Dote autois...phagein*] (Mark 6:37). Mark does not use Septuagint vocabulary; indeed he seems unaware that the bread is barley loaves (*artous krithinous*), calling it only unspecified "loaves" (*artous*). My point is that just as Mark is using Christian tradition, not eyewitness information, so is the Signs author, and they do so independently of each other. So even though we have in the Signs Gospel what Fortna calls "perhaps the earliest" of all gospels (Miller, 1992, 177), it is still at the third or fourth remove from the historical Jesus.

That the Signs author was indeed a Jewish believer in Jesus, as Fortna argues, shows clearly in the "second sign," Jesus' healing at a distance of an official's son at Capernaum. Here is that account in Fortna's most recent reconstruction of the Signs Gospel:

> Then he set out for Capernaum, he and his mother and brothers and disciples. And there was an official whose son was sick in Capernaum. When he heard that Jesus was coming, he approached him and pleaded with him: "Sir, please come down before my child dies." Jesus says, "Go, your son will live." And the man departed. While he was still

on his way home, his slaves met him and told him that his boy was alive. So he asked them when he had begun to recover, and they told him, "Yesterday at one o'clock the fever broke." Then the father realized that it was precisely the time Jesus had said to him, "Your son will live." So he believed. (Miller, 1992, 182-183)

Living as he did in the context of the synagogue, the Signs author would have known stories about wonder-rabbis. There is one about Rabbi Hanina ben Dosa that is strikingly similar to this account:

Once a son of Rabban Gamaliel (II) was ill. He sent two disciples to R. Hanina b. Dosa, that he might pray mercy for him. When he (b. Dosa) saw them, he went up to the attic and implored mercy for him. When he came down, he said to them, "Go, for the fever has left him."…They returned and noted the hour in writing. When they came back to Rabban Gamaliel he said to them:…"It happened exactly so; in that hour the fever left him." (Quoted in Barrett, 1978, 249)

Fortna does not cite this story, though doing so would have strengthened his thesis about the Judaism of the Signs author.

If, in fulfillment of Jewish hopes, Jesus was to be both another Moses and another Elijah/Elisha, he must not only miraculously provide food as did Moses with manna and Elijah with never-empty jars of flour and oil and as did Elisha with multiplying barley loaves, he must also miraculously transform water, as did Moses. The third "sign" certifying Moses before Israel was his ability to turn water into blood (Ex. 4:9). That Jesus in fact transformed water into wine—symbolic blood—shows the remarkably complex and cosmopolitan heritage of the story in John chapter two, an account that combines the biblical legend of Elijah's miraculous provision of food with a miracle of the Greek god Dionysus. Moreover, the water/blood symbolism implicit in this story is the first foreshadowing of the Crucifixion, when Jesus' side flowed both "blood and water" (John 19:34). We can best grasp the origins of this story by analyzing it as it now stands in the Fourth Gospel, rather than in Fortna's reconstruction, which leaves out some key words:

On the third day there was a wedding at Cana-in-Galilee. The mother of Jesus was there, and Jesus and his disciples were guests also. The wine gave out, so Jesus' mother said to him, "They have no wine left." He answered, "Woman, what have I to do with you? My hour is not yet come." His mother said to the servants, "Do whatever he tells you." There were six stone water-jars standing near... Jesus said to the servants, "Fill the jars with water," and they filled them to the brim... The steward tasted the water now turned into wine, not knowing its source, though the servants who had drawn the water knew. He hailed the bridegroom and said, "Everyone serves the best wine first, and waits until the guests have drunk freely before serving the poorer sort; but you have kept the best wine till now." (John 2:1-10)

Like the feeding of the five thousand, this story takes the Jewish part of its origin from Septuagint III Kings, where Elijah provides a "jar" (*hydria*) of flour that would always be full (III Kings 17:14 LXX), just as Jesus provides six "*jars*" (*hydriai*) of water changed to wine (John 2:6). Only on the basis of the Septuagint story of Elijah and the woman he helps can we understand the puzzling interchange between Jesus and his mother; for when she tells him "They have no wine," he answers with what seems like profound rudeness: "What have I to do with you, woman [*ti emoi kai soi, gynai*]?" (John 2:4). But this story is not an account of actual events; it is not rudeness reported, but prophecy fulfilled. For the woman (*gynē*) whom Elijah is about to help says to him "*ti emoi kai soi*" ("what have I to do with you?" (III Kings 17:18 LXX). Jesus is momentarily reluctant to provide his wine as symbolic blood because his "hour has not yet come"; but nonetheless, "in fulfillment of Scripture" (John 19:28), he calls for jars filled with water (*hydor*) (John 2:9), just as Elijah had called for a vessel of water (*hydor*) (III Kings 17:10 LXX). In John the water becomes wine in abundance, just as in III Kings the jar of flour never ran empty. But why jars of wine, instead of flour? Here the Greek myth of the god of wine, Dionysus, provides another clue to the origins of this Christian story in a cosmopolitan Greek-speaking city; as Rudolf Bultmann pointed out long ago, this story in the Fourth Gospel has a partly pagan origin: "On the festival day of Dionysus the temple springs of Andros and Teos were supposed every year to yield wine instead of water. In Elis on the eve of the feast, three empty pitchers were put into the temple and in the morning they were full of wine" (Bultmann, 1971, 238).

I shall not linger here over the third "sign" in John that has a close Synoptic parallel, the Miraculous Catch of Fish (John 21; Luke 5), because I am not convinced it comes from the Signs Gospel. I regard it as the work of "John 2," as I shall argue in the next chapter. Fortna himself admits that "assignment of this story to the [Signs] source is more hypothetical than for the other narratives," and that he only "provisionally" places it in the Signs Gospel, agreeing that "we can speculate" that it was the "post-Johannine redactor" (whom I call John 2) who "found such a story in a miracle tradition/source" and used it in John 21 (Fortna, 1988, 66-68).

Though it is at least arguable that the Signs author was dependent upon oral tradition about Jesus in the two or three miracle stories he shares with the Synoptics, this becomes quite clear when we examine the most striking of the "signs," the resurrection of Lazarus. There are now no parallels to this story in any of the Synoptic Gospels—but amazingly there was at one time, as has recently been discovered. An earlier, "secret" version of the Gospel of Mark (Koester, 1990, 302), now totally lost except for one quotation in a letter written by Clement of Alexandria about the year 200 C.E., contained a story that is clearly a variant of what became the "sign" of Lazarus. This story and its implications can tell us much about how the Signs author wrote.

The existence of a "version of the Gospel of Mark that was in use in Alexandria at least by the first quarter of the second century" and that contains passages not found in canonical Mark was not known about until 1958, when "Morton Smith discovered a fragment of a previously unknown letter of Clement of Alexandria (ca. 150-215 C.E.). This letter fragment mentions the Secret Gospel and contains two excerpts from this mysterious text" (Miller, 1992, 402). The most readily available translation of Secret Mark is that by Helmut Koester in *The Complete Gospels*; here from that translation are the opening sentences of what Clement preserves of this lost gospel:

> And they come into Bethany, and this woman was there whose brother had died. She knelt down in front of Jesus and says to him, "Son of David, have mercy on me." But the

disciples rebuked her. And Jesus got angry and went with her into the garden where the tomb was. Just then a loud voice was heard from inside the tomb. Then Jesus went up and rolled the stone away from the entrance to the tomb. He went right in where the young man was, stuck out his hand, grabbed him by the hand, and raised him up. (Miller, 1992, 405)

We can imagine Morton Smith's excitement in 1958 on first examining Clement's letter and grasping not only that he was reading part of an early version of Mark that no one knew existed, but also, as he wrote in 1973 (95): "As soon as I read the manuscript I saw that the resurrection story in it was a variant of the story of Lazarus" in John chapter eleven. So the Signs author knew a variant of a miracle story otherwise found only in a "secret" version of Mark that was shown to no one except Christian initiates in Alexandria who were "advancing with respect to knowledge [*gnosis*]," as Clement noted in his letter (Miller, 1992, 403). This does not mean that the Signs author was dependent on the Secret Gospel of Mark (there are no close verbal parallels between the two stories), but it does mean that the Signs author knew a miracle story that as far as we can tell circulated only in Alexandria. How the narrative in Secret Mark originated is not hard to show: it is a revision of stories in the Books of Kings about Elijah's and Elisha's resurrection miracles. In Secret Mark, the unnamed woman of Bethany comes to Jesus, falls at his feet and begs for mercy; just as in II Kings the unnamed woman of Shunnam came to Elisha and "clutched his feet," begging for his help. Elisha's disciple tries to prevent her unseemly touching of the prophet: "Gehazi came forward to push her away" (II Kings 4:27), just as Jesus' disciples "rebuked her" for approaching him. In both cases the prophets respond with anger, not at the importuning woman but at their followers who try to keep her away: Elisha says "Let her alone" (II Kings 4:27), while Jesus became "angry and went with her." In both stories the prophet follows the grieving woman to the place where her dead one lies, and in both the prophet touches the dead one somewhat roughly: Elisha "crouched upon him," as the Hebrew of II Kings 4:35 literally says; Jesus "grabbed him." In both stories the dead one makes a loud or explosive noise: the "boy sneezed seven times" (II Kings 4:35); a "loud voice" was heard in Secret Mark. And in both the dead arise and are presented to their loved ones. That the Secret Mark story originated in oral tradition that blended Elijah material with the Elisha model is clear in that when Elijah resurrects the dead son of an unnamed woman at Sarepta, "the child cried out" (I Kings 17:23), an event repeated closely in Secret Mark with a "loud voice" from the tomb.

This much is clear. But if, as seems to be the case, the Signs author knew a version of this narrative and repeated it as the resurrection of Lazarus, whence came the other details—such as the names Mary and Martha and Lazarus—and others that give such dramatic power to the scene in the Fourth Gospel? And where did the Signs author find such a narrative? We need to begin with the story itself. Here is Fortna's reconstruction:

> Now there was a certain [Mary] (and her sister Martha) of Bethany, whose brother Lazarus was sick. So she [or the sisters] sent to Jesus, saying, "Master, your beloved friend is sick." He said to the disciples, "Lazarus our friend has fallen asleep; let us go to him."
>
> So Jesus came, and found him already four days buried. (Now Bethany was near Jerusalem, about two miles away.) When Mary saw [Jesus], she fell at his feet and said to him, "Master, if you had been here my brother would not have died." So Jesus (when he saw her weeping) was angered in spirit and deeply troubled. And he said, "Where have you laid him?" They said to him, "Master, come and see." So Jesus came to the tomb. Now it was a cave, and had a stone lying against it. Jesus said, "Take away the stone." So they took the stone away. And Jesus (lifted up his eyes and) called out with a great cry, "Lazarus, come forth!" The dead man came forth, bound feet and hands with cloths, and his face wrapped in a handkerchief. Jesus said to them, "Unbind him and let him go." (Fortna, 1988, 94-95.)

As the brackets and parentheses show, Fortna is quite tentative in his reconstruction. He doesn't know for sure whether the Signs story has one woman or two, nor does he know if the women are weeping, or if Bethany needs identifying to the readers of the Signs Gospel. The uncertainty stems, he says, from the "highly complex textual problems in these verses," including the "hopelessly tangled problem of the source's view of the relationship among the three characters introduced at the story's opening" (i.e., was Martha there, was she Mary's sister, and was she also the sister of Lazarus?) (Fortna, 1988, 94). Fortna knows about Morton Smith's discovery of the Secret Gospel of Mark, but discounts that gospel as "having little bearing on the pre-Johannine source" since the Secret Gospel text, in his view, is in fact "derivative from the Synoptics and 4G [Fourth Gospel]" (Fortna, 1988, 94). Fortna has it backwards here; what he does not know is that the Signs author (or the tradition behind him) combined the Alexandrian tradition, based on the Books of Kings, of Jesus' resurrecting a young man, with yet another Egyptian myth to produce the story of Lazarus; that myth is the resurrection of King Osiris by the god Horus. Using this other source we can account for the details in the Signs story Fortna finds so difficult.

We have seen already that the Signs author knew a miracle story about the resurrection of a young man that, as far as we can tell, was revealed only to Christian initiates in Alexandria. I shall now argue that the Signs author wrote there, in Egypt, since he or his source employed the story of Osiris, an Egyptian myth that, says Wallis Budge, is "found inscribed upon tombs, sarcophagi, coffins, stelae and papyri from the XIth dynasty to about A.D. 200." In Egypt, "in texts of all periods, the life, sufferings, death and resurrection of Osiris are accepted as facts" (Budge, 1967, ix). The individual elements of the Osiris myth known to the Signs author (or the oral tradition behind him) are most readily available to us in R.O. Faulkner, *The Ancient Egyptian Pyramid Texts*, centuries older than the time of the Signs author, but as Budge has noted, "The chief features of the Egyptian religion remained unchanged from the Vth and VIth dynasties down to the period when the Egyptians embraced Christianity" (1969, xlix). Using Faulkner's edition of these texts we can watch the Secret Gospel story, set at Bethany, of the resurrection of an unnamed young man, become the Signs Gospel story of the resurrection of Lazarus. In the Egyptian myth, the god-king Osiris has two sisters, Isis and Nephthys. Osiris dies and is buried in the Egyptian necropolis of Annu (now a suburb of Cairo). In Egypt, this city had a variety of formulaic names: the

VII: *Who Wrote the Gospel of John, and How Did They Do It?*

"great house of Anu" (Budge, 1972, 124), "the mansion of the Prince in On" (Faulkner, 1969, 164); and in Greek it was known as Heliopolis, "City of the Sun." The Hebrew Bible mentions both the last two names: Joseph married a daughter of a priest at On (Gen. 41:45), while Jeremiah declared that Yahweh would "smash the sacred pillars of Beth-Shemesh ['House of the Sun']" (Jer. 43:13). That "City of the Sun" could be Semitized as "House of the Sun" is our first clue to the relationship of these two stories, pagan Egyptian and Christian Egyptian. Just as Heliopolis became "House of the Sun [Beth-Shemesh]," so the "House of Anu" could become Semitized as (in Greek letters) *Bethanu*. The village of Bethany near Jerusalem was already important in Secret Mark and the tradition behind it as a site of Jesus' activity, so it became the link between the two stories. Just as the "body of the Aged One, a name of Osiris, reposed in Annu" (Budge,1972, cxxxiv), Lazarus would die and be buried at *Bethanu*. Fortna's uncertainty over whether the Signs Gospel had two sisters mourning their dead brother can be overcome with the story's source in the Egyptian myth: "they come to Osiris the King at the sound of the weeping of Isis, at the cry of Nephthys" (Faulkner, 1969, Utterance 670). The Secret Gospel story concerns a nameless young man; Egyptian Jewish-Christian tradition could easily supply the name Lazarus, the Greek form of the Hebrew El-azar ("God Helps"), on the analogy of the god Osiris (in Hebrew, "El-Osiris"), yielding the development El-Osiris/El-azar/Lazarus.

The Egyptian myth relates of the dead Osiris in the house of Annu: "O Osiris the King, you have gone, but you will return; you have slept, [but you will awake]; you have died, but you will live" (Faulkner, 1969, Utterance 670; square brackets are the translator's). So Fortna need not have dropped the last part of John 11:11 from his reconstruction: "Our friend Lazarus has fallen asleep, but I shall go and wake him." To the dead Osiris, the god Horus says, "The tomb is opened for you, the doors of the tomb-chamber are thrown open for you" (Faulkner, Utterance 665A). This is the origin of Jesus' dramatic saying, "Take away the stone" (John 11:39). Again, Fortna need not have deleted Martha's dramatic statement to Jesus, "Sir, by now there will be a stench; he has been there four days"

(John 11:39), for the myth of Osiris that lies behind the Signs Gospel has it that "Osiris speaks to Horus, for he has removed the evil [which was on the King] on his fourth day" (Faulkner, 1969, Utterance 670). Indeed, Horus has already said to the dead Osiris, "O flesh of the king, do not decay, do not rot, do not smell unpleasant" (Faulkner, 1969, Utterance 412). The puzzling passage in the Secret Gospel of Mark about the "loud voice" from inside the tomb of the nameless young man becomes in the Signs Gospel Jesus' calling "out with a great cry, 'Lazarus, come forth!'" a much more dramatic line based on Horus' cry "Go forth, wake up" (Faulkner, 1969, Utterance 620). And again, the highly dramatic scene in the Signs Gospel where "the dead man came forth, bound hand and feet with cloths, and his face wrapped in a handkerchief," evoking Jesus' command "Unbind him and let him go," we can now trace to Utterance 703 in the Pyramid Texts: "O King, live, for you are not dead. Horus will come to you that he may cut your cords and throw off your bonds; Horus has removed your hindrance."

For the Signs author, the resurrection of Lazarus was only the fifth of the seven signs, according to Fortna; but in the Fourth Gospel, the story of Lazarus is the final "sign," the one that becomes the excuse for the Jewish authorities to seek Jesus' death. In preparing for the next chapter, we can now begin to see the differences between the Signs author and the writer who revised and absorbed his work, the great writer we call John. Fortna proposes, I think correctly, a date "in the 40s or possibly the 50s" for the Signs Gospel (Fortna, 1988, 216). This was still a time when the Second Coming of Jesus was expected imminently by misguided apocalyptic Christians like Paul (as in I Thess. 4:15), and when no one could have known about the approaching disaster of 70 C.E., when Roman armies destroyed Jerusalem and its temple. But John revised the Signs Gospel near the end of the first century, when the delay of the Second Coming had become a distinct embarrassment and when even the destruction of Jerusalem had not precipitated the apocalypse. We can date the Fourth Gospel on the basis of John 9:22: "the Jewish authorities had already agreed that anyone who acknowledged Jesus as Messiah should be banned from the synagogue." Now this event did not in fact occur until the second half of the eighties, as we know from the so-called "Heretic Benediction." In its "earliest form (as propounded by Samuel the Small for Rabban Gamaliel (A.D. 85-90)," says Barrett, "it must have run somewhat as follows: For the renegade let there be no hope, and may the arrogant kingdom soon be rooted out in our days, and the Nazarenes and the *minim* perish in a moment and be blotted out from the book of life and with the righteous may they not be inscribed." (Barrett, 1978, 362)

Barrett concludes that this "benediction was probably intended as a means of marking out Jewish Christians and excluding them from the synagogue community" (362). On this basis we can conclude that it was John, during the nineties, who added a new and profoundly ironic conclusion to the story of Lazarus he found in the Signs Gospel; for whereas the earlier work blames official condemnation of Jesus on his Sabbath-day healings, John says it was the raising of Lazarus that caused the High Priest to call for his execution:

> Now many of the Jews who had come to visit Mary and had seen what Jesus did put their faith in him. But some of them went off to the Pharisees and reported what he had done. Thereupon the chief priests and the Pharisees convened a meeting of the Council. "What action are we taking?" they said. "This man is performing many signs. If we leave him alone like this the whole populace will believe in him. Then the Romans will come and sweep away our temple and our nation." (John 11:47-48)

John's irony is bitter; by his time, the whole populace had *not* come to believe, and yet Jerusalem and its temple had been destroyed anyway. This passage only makes sense placed a good while after 70, when Christianity was rapidly becoming a gentile religion, and when Jerusalem had long since been destroyed, belying the misguided hope of those like Mark that the city's destruction meant the imminence of the Second Coming. The reviser of the Signs Gospel wrote in part to re-interpret the idea of the Second Coming and to explain the failure of Jesus to return soon after 70; and he wrote, I have speculated, in Alexandria, whose Jewish-Christian community had long used the Signs Gospel.

I argue the Alexandrian provenance of John's Gospel on the basis of the following: We know that in Alexandria there were at least three different versions of the Gospel of Mark in use—(1) ordinary Mark, (2) an expanded "Secret Mark," containing the story of Jesus' resurrecting a young man who loved him, a version of Mark shown only to fully initiated Christians in Alexandria, and (3) an even further expanded version of Mark used by a sect of Gnostic Christians called Carpocratians, who were the subject of Clement's letter discovered by Morton Smith. One of those who knew the story, found in Secret Mark and presumably in Carpocratian Mark, of Jesus' resurrection of the young man, was the author of the Gospel of Signs. Thus a good case can be made that this gospel was written in Alexandria. Now, if such conservative scholars of the Fourth Gospel as Raymond Brown are correct in their view that the hypothetical document called the Signs Gospel in fact never existed, then this work drops out of the equation and the strong case can be made that the Gospel of John was written in Alexandria, using Secret Mark or the tradition behind it as a source. Even if Brown is wrong (and I think he is), and John did indeed use the Signs Gospel as a written source, John's connection with Alexandria remains quite strong. We know that Alexandrian Christians had a very high regard for the Gospel of John; indeed the very first commentary ever written on this gospel was produced in Alexandria early in the second century by a Gnostic Christian named Heracleon (see Elaine Pagels' pioneering work, *The Johannine Gospel in Gnostic Exegesis*). If John did indeed revise the Signs Gospel in Alexandria, this will be the starting point of the next chapter.

VIII

The Mind of John

A GOOD CASE CAN BE MADE THAT THE SIGNS GOSPEL was the gospel of Alexandrian Jews who accepted Jesus as Messiah. It would have worked very well in the fifties, sixties and seventies of the first century, being used to demonstrate, from the Septuagint, that the Messiah had come, a coming proved by the "signs and wonders" Jesus had performed, as "predicted" in Scripture. Robert Fortna argues that not long after the Signs Gospel was written it was joined with a Passion/Resurrection narrative to form a gospel of the Synoptic type, in which crucifixion, resurrection and ascension formed the prelude to a Second Coming in the near future. Such a gospel would have worked very well in Alexandria in the seventies, when the city was flooded with Jewish refugees from the Jewish War in Palestine who would welcome apocalyptic hopes.

We know very little about first-century Alexandrian Christianity aside from a fascinating story in the Book of Acts showing Luke's conviction that Alexandria was home to a thoroughly obsolete kind of Jewish Christianity, one that knew neither Christian baptism nor the glossolalia that was so central to her understanding of the new religion. Luke tells us that "There arrived at Ephesus a Jew named Apollos, an Alexandrian by birth, an eloquent man, powerful in his use of the scriptures. He had been instructed in the way of the Lord and was full of spiritual fervor; and in his discourses he taught accurately the facts about Jesus, though the only baptism he knew was John's.... Priscilla and Aquila...took him in hand and expounded the way to him in greater detail" (Acts 18:24-26).

Even though Apollos was "instructed in the way of the Lord" he knew nothing of Christian baptism; his version of Christianity was limited to "demonstrating from the scriptures that the Messiah is Jesus" (Acts 18:20).

In other words, Apollos of Alexandria preached the Jewish Christianity of the Signs Gospel, a set of beliefs that Luke, writing around 100 C.E., regarded as standing outside the developing Pauline mainstream and needing to be brought up to date. The kind of Christianity that came to Ephesus from Alexandria knew neither baptism "in Jesus" nor "tongues of ecstasy" (Acts 19:2,6) until the missionary companions of Paul showed it the light. In the next chapter I shall argue how important this passage from Alexandria to Ephesus was in the history of the Fourth Gospel.

By the time she wrote Acts, in Luke's view Alexandrian Christianity was already out of date, being too "Jewish," though such a form of Christianity could have survived in Alexandria until 117 C.E., when the Jewish community there was virtually annihilated (Eusebius, 1960, 4.2). But already by the end of the eighties, I shall argue, it had become clear to at least one Christian, John, that the Signs Gospel had outlived its usefulness and had to be either revised or replaced. Several converging facts made this clear. The first was the introduction into Alexandria of the Gospel of Mark, a gospel written by and for gentile Christians and carrying with it (being from Syria) the authority of that area between Antioch and Damascus that recognized the primacy of Peter. After the destruction of Jerusalem in 70, gentile Christianity—the religion promulgated by Paul and by the Gospel of Mark—seemed clearly the wave of the future, and had to be accommodated, even in Alexandria. According to Eusebius, Mark, the interpreter of Peter, came to Alexandria soon after Peter's death and became the first Bishop of that city (1960, 2.16). Though this is Christian legend based on the apocryphal *Acts of Mark,* we may nonetheless take it to mean, at the very least, that the Gospel of Mark was introduced into Alexandria not long after it was written in Syria; some time in the eighties seems a good guess, since by the first quarter of the second century it had already effloresced into at least three different versions, as we know from Clement's letter cited above.

The second converging fact was the expulsion of Jewish Christians from the synagogue as a consequence of the "'Heretic Benediction" promulgated in the second half of the eighties, part of Judaism's struggle to re-define itself after the disaster of 70 (Barrett, 1978, 362); as John has Jesus say, "They will ban you from the synagogue" (John 6:2). So by the end of the eighties, a gospel by Jews for Jews to prove Jesus the Jewish Messiah had become superfluous, and Christianity was spreading among gentiles, even in Alexandria. The third and perhaps most important converging fact in John's view was the delay of the *Parousia*, the failure of apocalyptic expectations in the generation after the year 70. These three, working in the mind of a very great religious genius, called forth the first edition of the Gospel of John. This chapter will attempt to increase the confidence behind Elaine Pagels' assertion: "Most scholars believe that John wrote his Gospel, perhaps in Alexandria, about a generation after the war, c. 90-95 C.E." (1995, 8).

In Alexandria, I shall argue, at about the time Matthew was writing his gospel, John was mulling over the Signs Gospel and deciding it badly needed revision. He became convinced that even though it told true stories about Jesus, it failed to understand the real meaning of those stories. Note that this attitude toward the Signs Gospel is precisely analogous to Matthew's and Luke's attitudes toward the Gospel of Mark. Matthew, for example, believed that though Mark correctly quoted the parable of the Sower and the Seed, he misunderstood the purpose of parables, thinking that they were intended to conceal the gospel message from those "outside" (Mark 4:11). Likewise John also believed that the Signs Gospel misunderstood the purpose of "signs," for "the Evangelist made use of a source whose theological message differed from his own." While this source "attempts to represent Jesus throughout as someone legitimated by miracles" (Haenchen, 1984, I, 77), John was convinced that belief in Jesus because of "signs" was an inadequate basis for the religious life: "Will none of you ever believe without seeing signs and portents?" (John 4:48). "Signs and portents" had traditionally been understood as evidence that the "last days" were at hand. As Luke has Peter say at Pentecost, paraphrasing Joel chapter two: 'This will happen in the last days [*eschatais hēmerais*]...I will show portents in the sky above, and signs on the earth below" (Acts 2:17). For Luke, such "signs and portents" referred to Jesus, "a man singled out by God and made known to you through miracles, portents, and signs" (Acts 2:22). A Jesus presented as a purveyor of "signs" was a Jesus seen in the light of this kind of eschatological thinking. But John had a totally different understanding not only of "signs" but of eschatology, and this is part of what lies behind his revision of the Signs Gospel. John believed that "future eschatology"—the hope that someday soon Jesus would return and complete his task—failed to grasp Jesus' greatness and accomplishment. As Willi Marxsen, following Bultmann, has pointed out, in the Gospel of John the main thrust is toward a "denial of the hope of the *Parousia*, on the grounds that the first coming of Jesus was the decisive event and no further coming, no further judgment, is to be expected" (Marxsen, 1968, 262). John insists, for example, that Martha misses the point when she expects her brother Lazarus to "rise again at the resurrection on the last day [*eschatē hēmerai*]." Rather, as Jesus tells her, "I am the resurrection and the life" (John 11:25-26). John is attempting a very radical revision of the kind of eschatology first-century Christians had previously held, and he repeats again and again his effort to do so. For John resurrection, judgment and assignment to eternal life are not a matter for the future, because "death" (now become a mere metaphor) has become a matter of the past: "no one who is alive and has faith shall ever die" (John 11:26). "Death" is what one is in *now* if one is not born again; eternal life is what one has now if one *has* been born again (John 3:3). Jesus has rendered a future judgment day forever superfluous, for "The man who puts faith in him does not come under judgment; but the unbeliever has already been judged" (John 3:18). It is not that we *will be* judged: our life is our judgment, and eternal life is life already possessed by believers: "anyone who gives heed to what I say and puts his trust in him who sent me has hold of eternal life, and does not come up for judgment, but has already passed from death to life" (John 5:24).

Judgment is not a *future* matter but a matter of (John's) past, the "now" of Jesus: "Now is the hour of judgment for this world; now shall the Prince of this world be driven out" (John 12:31). It was the person and acts of Jesus himself that were the eschatological moment; resurrection is not ahead, but behind and now, in the eternal present of the believer: "a time is coming, indeed it is already here, when the dead shall hear the voice of

VIII: The Mind of John

the Son of God, and all who hear shall come to life" (John 5:25). No one should be surprised that Egyptian gnostics like Heracleon held the Gospel of John in such high regard (Pagels, 1973, 3).

For John, Jesus' moment of total triumph is not some future Second Coming; rather his triumph has already happened at the Crucifixion/glorification (which John turned into a single great moment): "I shall draw all men to myself when I am lifted up from the earth" (John 12:32). "The Son of Man must be lifted up as the serpent was lifted up by Moses in the wilderness, so that everyone who has faith in him may in him possess eternal life," (John 3:14-15). This is why John deliberately changed the traditional dying words of Jesus (preserved in Mark and Matthew) that had been borrowed from Psalm 22—"My God, my God, why hast thou forsaken me?"—to a cry of triumph: "It is accomplished!" (John 19:30).

Now John did not do all this revision of traditional eschatological notions in a vacuum; indeed, the failure of Jesus to return was about to exercise the wits of Matthew and Luke as well, as they pondered the theological blunders of the Gospel of Mark, which had been written under the misguided belief that "some of those [personal associates of Jesus] standing here will not taste death before they have seen the kingdom of God already come in power" (Mark 9:1). When that self-disconfirming prophecy necessarily proved wrong, and Jesus' whole generation died, it had to be reinterpreted. Such a task fell, a generation or so after Mark, to the authors of Matthew and Luke, whose works express the theme of the "delay of the *Parousia*": that the Second Coming would be a bit later than Mark had expected. Luke argues that it was only misguided Christians in Jesus' time who "thought that the reign of God might dawn at any moment" (19:11), for Jesus had explicitly warned them about a "long journey abroad" before he could be "appointed king and then return" (19:12). Even after the Resurrection, says Luke, some misguided Christians still had not yet understood that the *Parousia* and the kingdom would be delayed: "They asked him, 'Lord, is this the time when you are to establish the sovereignty of Israel?'" In response Jesus tells them not to ask such questions: "It is not for you to know about dates and times"; rather, they should instead busy themselves fulfilling their commission to "bear witness for me...to the ends of the earth" (Acts 1:7-8). Essentially Matthew employs the same method of re-interpreting Mark: Yes, it was true that "the master is a long time coming" (Matt. 24:48), sadly it was so that the "bridegroom was late in coming" (Matt. 25:5); but this does not mean that the master, the bridegroom, is *not* coming. No: "the master will arrive on a day [you] do not expect" (Matt. 24:50), the bridegroom will indeed appear, but at "midnight," when many are asleep (Matt. 25:10). Therefore the delay should not move Christians to complacency: "Keep awake, then; for you never know the day or the hour" (Matt. 25:13).

Though the Gospel of John is not based on Mark in the way that Matthew and Luke are, its author nevertheless saw and pondered the failure of Christian expectations about the return of Jesus. But whereas Matthew and Luke deal with that failure simply by stretching out the period between Resurrection and return ("a long time"), John used a totally different method; in the Fourth Gospel, the *delay* of the *Parousia* is modulated into the *redundancy* of the *Parousia*. In the work of John, it is not that the Son of Man is *about* to come, but that the Son of Man has *already come and gone*, the eschatological event has already happened in the person of Jesus himself: "No one ever went up into heaven except the one who came down from heaven, the Son of Man whose home is in heaven" (John 3:13). For this author, the eschatological hope that the "son of man" would come from "heaven" to receive "glory and kingly power" (a hope based on Daniel 7:13), had *already been fulfilled*! It is hard to overestimate the originality of a mind that could turn the *failure* of eschatological hopes into the *fulfillment* of eschatological hopes.

The author we call John tried very hard to cure Christianity of the religious illusion known technically as "future eschatology"; his effort at a cure has come to be known, after C.H. Dodd, as "realized eschatology"—that the person and acts of Jesus were themselves all that was necessary for the salvation of the world (Dodd, 1961). To look to future eschatology is implicitly to argue the incompetence of Jesus, that he needs to come back in order to finish his work, while realized eschatology fully accepts Jesus' final cry of triumph: "It is accomplished!" (John 19:30). Indeed, ever since the groundbreaking commentary on the Fourth Gospel by Rudolf Bultmann (first published in 1941 as *Das Evangelium des Johannes*), it has become widely accepted that "John", the anonymous reviser of the Signs Gospel, no longer expected any apocalyptic events in the future, since God's decisive offer of salvation through faith in Jesus was all that was needed. As it happened, however, John's attempt to re-define eschatology was so radical that it failed (being smothered over by John 2, who re-introduced future eschatology back into the Fourth Gospel, as we shall see in the next chapter); and sadly the effect of this re-introduction has been that much of contemporary Christianity remains saddled with an always self-disconfirming claim ("Jesus is coming soon").

Synoptic Christianity, arriving in Alexandria in (perhaps) the eighties in the form of the Gospel of Mark, a gospel thought to bear Petrine authority, threatened to render the Christianity of the Signs Gospel passé, as outdated as Luke saw it when Paul encountered it at Ephesus (Acts 18). Part of the reason for John's effort to replace the Signs Gospel with his own was John's response to the revolutionary intrusion of Synoptic Christianity into Alexandria, with its high view of Peter's role among the disciples. While the Synoptics put Peter at the center of the Twelve ("You are Peter; and on this rock I will build my church" [Matt. 16:18]), John consistently downgrades Peter. While Mark names Simon Peter first among the apostles, making him the original Christian, the very first to answer Jesus' call (Mark 1:16), John names Simon only second, after his brother Andrew, and makes Andrew the initiator, the one who first calls Jesus the Christ and who brings Simon to Jesus only later with the words "We have found the Messiah" (John 1:41). In the Synoptics, by contrast, it is Peter who is given the honor of first calling Jesus the Messiah (Mark 8:29; Matt. 16:16; Luke 9:20). Peter becomes the laggard in the Fourth Gospel, not the impetuous first follower as in the Synoptics. This becomes especially apparent at the Last Supper, when John introduces into world literature a new and profoundly mysterious character,

Who Wrote The Gospels?

the Beloved Disciple.

The Beloved Disciple is mysterious because of his anonymity, a name-lessness deliberate on John's part. John does not *want* us to know the name of this figure, a ploy that suggests he is John's fictional creation, as Bultmann (1971), Kaesemann (1968), and others have suggested. Whether this figure is indeed purely John's invention remains controversial, but his function in this gospel is perfectly clear: every time the Beloved Disciple appears in the first twenty chapters of John, his presence is a direct or an implied rebuke to the authority of Peter as the First Christian, the "Rock" of the church. The Beloved Disciple is John's tool for downgrading Peter, that is, for downgrading Petrine Christianity, the Christianity of the Gospel of Mark.

John's revision of the Signs Gospel was offered as competition to the Gospel of Mark in Alexandria; but it failed in this goal among all Christians in Egypt except the Gnostics, who joyfully accepted it as confirming their interpretation of Jesus. I will argue that later; for now, back to the Beloved Disciple. He first appears at the Last Supper, in a story John offers as deliberate challenge to the account of Mark. While Mark presented the Last Supper as a Passover meal during which Jesus instituted a new, Christian ritual—the Eucharist—to replace the old Jewish one, John explicitly denies that the Last Supper was a Passover, arguing that in fact it happened the *night before* Passover (John 13:1; 18:8). John had, in fact, little interest in any Christian ritual except foot-washing, and being a Jewish Christian only reluctantly separated from the synagogue he had a high regard for Passover. In his account of the Last Supper John not only substitutes foot-washing ritual for Eucharist ritual, he even implicitly denigrates the Eucharist by presenting Judas Iscariot as the only person to whom Jesus offers bread: this bread is for betrayers only! And even as bread is downgraded, so is Peter, presented as less intimate with Jesus than is the Beloved Disciple, who now reclines in Jesus' bosom:

> Jesus exclaimed in deep agitation of spirit, "In truth, in very truth I tell you, one of you is going to betray me." The disciples looked at one another in bewilderment: whom could he be speaking of? One of them, the disciple he loved, was reclining close beside Jesus. So

VIII: The Mind of John

Simon Peter nodded to him and said, "Ask who it is he means." That disciple, as he reclined, leaned back close to Jesus and asked, "Lord, who is it?" Jesus replied, "It is the man to whom I give this piece of bread when I have dipped it in the dish." Then, after dipping it in the dish, he took it out and gave it to Judas son of Simon Iscariot. (John 13:21-26)

Only John among the four gospels names Judas as a son of Simon (thus implicitly linking him with Simon Peter who will thrice deny Jesus this very night), and only John gives us this scene in which the figure closest to Jesus is not Peter but the Beloved Disciple, through whose intercession the identity of the betrayer is revealed; access to Jesus is through the Beloved Disciple, even for Peter. In John, the "Rock" is demoted among the Twelve at the Last Supper. This demotion continues in John's version of Jesus' interrogation before the High Priest Caiaphas.

John preserves the tradition, found in all four gospels, that on the night of Jesus' arrest Peter denied him three times, but in the Fourth Gospel he does so only by way of the intercession, again, of the mysterious Beloved Disciple, who becomes an even more mysterious figure in this scene, as John forces us to surmise that it is indeed he who sees to it that Peter is given the opportunity to fulfill Jesus' prediction of Peter's triple denial. After Jesus is arrested and taken to the courtyard of Caiaphas,

Jesus was followed by Simon Peter and another disciple [*allos mathētēs*]. This disciple, who was acquainted with the High Priest, went with Jesus into the High Priest's courtyard, but Peter halted at the door outside. So the other disciple, the High Priest's acquaintance, went out again and spoke to the woman at the door, and brought Peter in. The maid on duty at the door said to Peter, "Are you another of this man's disciples?" "I am not," he said. (John 18:15-17)

In John's work, Peter cannot even manage to *deny* his Lord without the prior assistance of the "other disciple", who, being acquainted with the High Priest, has entree to the official's courtyard. It is only in John's Greek vocabulary that we can identify this "other disciple" (*allos mathētēs*) who precedes Peter into the courtyard. He is in the lead, literally and figuratively, both here and in the twentieth chapter, when we can finally grasp who he is. There, Mary of Magdala, on finding Jesus' tomb empty,

> ran to Simon Peter and the other disciple [*allon mathētēn*], the one whom Jesus loved. "They have taken the Lord out of his tomb," she cried, "and we do not know where they have laid him." So Peter and the other disciple [*allos mathētēs*] set out and made their way to the tomb. They were running side by side, but the other disciple [*allos mathētēs*] outran Peter and reached the tomb first. (John 20:2-4)

So the "other disciple" is the "one whom Jesus loved," the one who takes precedence over Peter every time he appears in the first twenty chapters of John's gospel, the one who gives Peter access to the High Priest's courtyard and who outruns him to the empty tomb. Now we can understand the role of this "other", the Beloved Disciple, at the scene of Peter's denial of Jesus in the High Priest's courtyard. In forcing us to surmise his identity —that he is the Beloved Disciple—John is forcing us to interpret this scene: it is the perfect allegory, in John's work, for the relationship between Alexandrian Jewish Christianity and the "outside" Christianity of the Gospel of Mark. The "other disciple" has close connections with the Jewish hierarchy; being acquainted with the High Priest, he has access to the inner workings of Judaism in his city at the highest levels, while Peter, the outsider from the north, must accept his help and his precedence. Can there be a better allegory for John's view of his Alexandrian Jewish Christianity, which until quite recently had been granted access to the synagogue and the high councils of his city's Judaism, a Christianity that would, on sufferance, grant access into Alexandria to the alien, northern, Petrine Christianity of the Gospel of Mark? The Beloved Disciple is Alexandrian Jewish Christians, graciously accepting and helping the gentile Christianity of Mark, the gospel that was thought to bear the authority of Peter. Well, Peter *may* be behind Mark, but, says John, he is *certainly* "behind" the Beloved Disciple, to whom he must grant precedence. That precedence continues in chapter twenty, as the two disciples hurry toward the empty tomb:

> the other disciple outran Peter and reached the tomb first. He peered in and saw the linen wrappings lying there, but did not enter. Then Simon Peter came up, following

him, and he went into the tomb. He saw the linen wrappings lying, and the napkin
which had been over his head, not lying with the wrappings but rolled together in a
place by itself. Then the disciple who had reached the tomb first went in too, and he saw
and believed; until then they had not understood the scriptures, which showed that he
must rise from the dead. (John 20:4-9)

In John, the first to grasp that the empty tomb means the Resurrection
is the Beloved Disciple, not the women, as in the Synoptic Gospels, and
certainly not Peter (to whom the risen Jesus appeared first, according to I
Cor. 15:5 and Luke 24:34). But in John's version, the Beloved Disciple
"believed" first, before Peter, before Mary Magdalene; the Beloved
Disciple's Christianity is the *original* Christianity, according to John. He is,
indeed, the protector of faithful Jewish Christianity, the protector, that is,
of the mother of Jesus. John makes this clear in the final appearance of this
nameless disciple in his work, at the foot of the cross: "near the cross where
Jesus hung stood his mother, with her sister, Mary wife of Clopas, and
Mary of Magdala. Jesus saw his mother, with the disciple whom he loved
standing beside her. He said to her, 'Mother, there is your son'; and to the
disciple, 'There is your mother'; and from that moment the disciple took
her into his home" (John 19:25-27). Once again, the Beloved Disciple's
presence at the cross is an implicit rebuke to Peter; where was he?

One of the most striking and original strategies of John's Gospel is his
rendering nameless the mother of Jesus. How many readers notice that
John places three women (or perhaps four) at the foot of the cross, one (or
two) of them unnamed, two of them named Mary—and neither Mary is
Jesus' mother? John's deliberate ambiguity is almost playful here. Are there
four women—two named Mary, plus an anonymous pair (Jesus' nameless
mother and aunt)—or just three, Mary of Magdala, Jesus' aunt Mary wife
of Clopas, and Jesus' nameless mother (who would thus *not* be named
Mary, having already a sister of that name). Raymond Brown feels compelled to argue for four women, presumably not wanting to see John
imply that Jesus' mother was not named Mary (Brown, 1970, 904).
Indeed, Jesus' mother never is named in the Fourth Gospel; she is deliberately kept as anonymous as the Beloved Disciple himself, and for the same

reason: they both stand for groups of people, he for Alexandrian Jewish Christians, she for faithful Judaism, the matrix of Jesus that is now and forever under the care of the Beloved Disciple. As R. H. Strachan puts it, Jesus' mother here "represents the heritage of Israel that is now being entrusted to the Christians (the Beloved Disciple)" (Strachan, 1941, 319). In other words, John's strategy of rendering Jesus' mother nameless relates to his introduction of an unnamed Beloved Disciple; both are thematic functions as much as characters.

The Beloved Disciple represents John's own kind of Christianity, one that no longer expects a Second Coming but rather lives and worships "in spirit" (John 4:23), being guided by the "Advocate," the "spirit of truth" (John 14:16), whose eternal presence necessarily means Jesus' eternal absence: "It is for your good that I am leaving you. If I do not go, your Advocate will not come, whereas if I go, I will send him to you" (John 16:7).

Thus, for John, resurrection means Jesus' absence: "I am going away to him who sent me" (16:5). Now this is, of course, a very troubling idea to those who expect an imminent Second Coming, so John has to re-interpret what such an idea might mean. He does this most clearly in Jesus' farewell discourse in chapters thirteen through seventeen, when John heavily reshapes the meaning of that last night of Jesus' life. Haenchen is quite right in saying that the mind of John is most clearly revealed in Jesus' discourses in the Fourth Gospel (Haenchen 1984, 90). Those discourses show a great mind in the process of re-thinking the "obsolete" Christianity of the Signs Gospel as well as the already disconfirmed near-term future eschatology of such works as the Gospel of Mark.

Jesus' discourses in the Fourth Gospel are John's messages to the Christians of his own time, which we can date using John 16:2: "They will ban you from the synagogue," a process that began in the second half of the eighties (Barrett, 1978, 362). Not only were Jewish Christians excluded from the synagogue, but the Christian message was spreading rapidly to non-Jews as well, a group that had to be included now with Jewish Christians: "But it is not for these alone that I pray, but for those who through their words put their faith in me; may they all be one: as thou,

VIII: The Mind of John

Father, art in me and I in thee, so also may they be in us....that they may be one, as we are one" (John 17:20-23).

A major problem among those for whom Jesus prayed was the delay of the *Parousia*; for many had thought that the phrase "a little while, and you will see me" (John 16:16) implied an early Second Coming, and now some sixty years later this had not happened. Such a failure had caused divisions:

> Some of his disciples said to one another, "What does he mean by this: 'A little while, and you will see me', and by this: 'Because I am going to my Father'?" So they asked, "What is this little while that he speaks of? We do not know what he means." (John 16:17-18)

With great ingenuity, John changes the (mistakenly supposed) brief period between Jesus' death and Second Coming into the (truly) brief period between Jesus' death and resurrection:

> Jesus knew that they were wanting to question him and said, "Are you discussing what I said: 'A little while, and you will not see me, and again a little while, and you will see me'? In very truth I tell you, you will weep and mourn, but the world will be glad. But though you will be plunged in grief, your grief will be turned to joy...For the moment you are sad at heart; but I shall see you again, and then you will be joyful, and no one shall rob you of your joy." (John 16:19-20)

"I shall see you again" becomes a prediction of the Resurrection, not of the *Parousia*; thus for John the coming of the Advocate after Jesus' departure takes the place of the Second Coming. And for John, Jesus' resurrection and the giving of the "Advocate," the Holy Spirit, happen on the same day. Just as Jesus had predicted in 16:20, when, after the Resurrection, "the disciples saw the Lord, they were filled with joy" (John 20:20). "Then he breathed on them, saying, 'Receive the Holy Spirit!'" (John 20:22). All this is the real meaning, for John, of the phrase "I am coming back to you" in Jesus' final discourse:

> If you love me, you will obey my commands; and I will ask the Father, and he will give you another to be your Advocate, who will be with you forever—the Spirit of Truth...I will not leave you bereft; I am coming back to you. In a little while, the world will see me no longer, but you will see me; because I live, you too will live; then you will know that I

am in my Father, and you in me and I in you....Anyone who loves me will heed
what I say; then my Father will love him, and we will come to him and make our
dwelling with him.... I have told you all this while I am still here with you; but your
Advocate, the Holy Spirit whom the Father will send in my name, will teach you everything, and will call to your mind all that I have told you." (John 14:15-21; 23-26).

Here John goes too far, and almost seems to identify *himself*—the one
who reveals to the disciples what Jesus *really* said on his last night—as the
promised Advocate. We begin to touch upon the reasons why John's work
became a lost gospel, why it could not be accepted by mainstream
Christianity until it was revised by John 2, and why it was so attractive to
Gnostic Christians in Alexandria. Demonstration of all this will serve as
the conclusion to the present chapter.

In arguing that the Resurrection and the giving of the Advocate takes
the place of the Second Coming—or rather *is* the Second Coming—that
"we will come to him and make our dwelling with him" "who loves me" is
the meaning of all future Christianity, John has placed his gospel on a trajectory that leads away from institutional orthodox Christianity and
toward a religion of personal inwardness in which the person in whom "I
and the Father" dwell is in some sense identical with the Father: "that they
may be one as we are one; I in them and thou in me, may be perfectly one"
(John 17:22). In a developed form, this kind of religion is called Christian
Gnosticism. Now Johannine scholarship has been unanimous in its rejec-
tion of Bultmann's notions that the revelation discourses in John were
borrowed from a Gnostic source (see, for example, Haenchen, 1984, I,
160) and that John was a convert to Christianity from some proto-gnostic group like the Mandaeans, the John-the-Baptist sect. Still, Luke regarded Alexandrian Christianity as a "John-the-Baptist" Christianity (Acts 18);
we need not accept Bultmann's notions in order to see why John's revision
of the Signs Gospel was so attractive to Alexandrian Gnostics like
Valentinus and Heracleon, both of whom used it extensively. A great deal
of what John wrote can be easily interpreted in a gnosticising fashion;
and until John's work was re-written to make such interpretation more

difficult, it could not be accepted by mainstream Christianity.

John presents a Jesus who is beyond the grasp—literally—of mortal men: "'I know him because I come from him and he it is who sent me.' At this they tried to seize him, but no one laid a hand on him because his appointed hour had not yet come" (John 7:29-30). Any docetic gnostic could read this and say "Aha! Of course no one could lay a hand on flesh that was only apparent, not real and substantial." And again when Jesus declares that "before Abraham was born, I am," "They picked up stones to throw at him, but Jesus was not to be seen," any docetic gnostic could say, "Of course, Jesus could materialize and de-materialize at will, as when he passed through a closed door in John 20:19." Remember that Epiphanius knew of Gnostic Christians who actually believed that the Gnostic teacher Cerinthus of Ephesus was the author of the Fourth Gospel! (*Adv. Haeres.* 51.3.6) In arguing against the too simple-minded Signs Gospel, John did indeed make Jesus sound like a Gnostic teacher who held that the flesh is of no use whatever, that only the spirit and those who are spiritualized really matter: "Flesh can give birth only to flesh; it is spirit that gives birth to spirit. You ought not to be astonished, then, when I tell you that you must be born over again. The wind blows where it wills; you hear the sound of it, but you do not know where it comes from, or where it is going. So with everyone who is born from spirit" (John 3:6-8).

This can easily be read, in tandem with "Jesus was not to be seen," to say that anyone born from spirit can likewise come and go unseen. John has Jesus declare unequivocally, "The spirit alone gives life; the flesh is of no avail" (John 6:63). If flesh is of no avail, and only those born over again from spirit can "see the kingdom of God" (John 3:3), how is it that Jesus could also say "whoever eats my flesh and drinks my blood possesses eternal life" (John 6:54)? How can John make Jesus call the Eucharist of no avail in one speech and essential in another? Modern scholarship has almost unanimously accepted, as Haenchen writes, the existence of a "later, 'conservative' editor," who "replaced [John's] 'now-eschatology' with the traditional futuristic eschatology—where the dead rise out of their graves—and again introduced the sacraments" (1984, I, 33). I think only thus can we explain the kinds of difficulties mentioned above. Luke was right—Alexandrian Christianity in the first century did not know about baptism "in Jesus" (Acts 19:4). For John's community, being born again was all that was required, not some institutionalized ritual of initiation. And for John's community, flesh is of no avail, so a ritual of eating flesh could in no way lead one to eternal life. Lack of institutional structure, denigration of ritual, denigration of flesh, inward spiritual experience of the individual, a Jesus who could be seen as more spirit than body—no wonder Gnostics welcomed John's Gospel, and no wonder it had to be re-written to be acceptable to the developing mainstream.

A look at one more passage in John—"I am the bread of life"—will indicate the kind of re-writing I mean. John's revisions of the Signs Gospel had consistently involved the addition of discourses by Jesus that re-interpret the meaning of his miracles to downplay the importance of faith based on "signs" and stress instead the importance of faith in Jesus without such carnal things as signs, which can be no more than pointers to the really important spiritual things. After the miracle of the loaves and fishes, Jesus addresses the still unbelieving crowd:

> "I know that you have not come looking for me because you saw signs, but because you ate the bread and your hunger was satisfied. You must work, not for this perishable food, but for the food that lasts, the food of eternal life. This food the Son of Man will give you…" "Then what must we do?" they asked him. Jesus replied, "Believe in the one whom he has sent." (John 6:26-29)

The crowd still does not understand or believe, so they ask him, "What sign can you give us to see, so that we may believe you?" Here John for once has become careless; in his haste to denigrate faith based on signs, he forgets that the crowd has already seen a stupendous sign, five thousand fed with five loaves and two fishes. The demand for a sign is here somewhat surprising; but John's point is that signs are merely pointers to God:

> "the truth is, not that Moses gave you the bread from heaven, but that my Father gives you the real bread from heaven. The bread that God gives comes down from heaven....I am the bread of life...I have come down from heaven."...At this, the Jews began to murmur

disapprovingly because he said, "I am the bread which came down from heaven." They said, "Surely this is Jesus son of Joseph; we know his father and mother. How can he now say, 'I have come down from heaven?'" (John 6:32,35,41)

Aware of the crowd's disapproval of his claim of arrival from heaven, Jesus goes further: "Does this shock you? What if you see the Son of Man ascending to the place where he was before? The spirit alone gives life; the flesh is of no avail; the words which I have spoken to you are both spirit and life" (John 6:62-63).

John's point is perfectly clear. Material things like bread and flesh are of no avail; only spirit matters. Jesus' return to heaven will validate his descent from heaven, and he came to give words of life, not bread of flesh. But John 2, who re-wrote the passage, added last-day eschatology and Eucharistic symbolism, turning Jesus' metaphors into literalisms. Whereas John's Jesus declares that whoever "comes" to him, "puts his faith in him," possesses "eternal life;" John 2 adds "and I will raise him up on the last day" (John 6:40). Whereas John had taken pains to stress that "Flesh is of no avail," John 2 adds, "whoever eats my flesh and drinks my blood possesses eternal life, and I will raise him up on the last day" (John 6:53-54). What is originally in John's work metaphorical and spiritual, expressive of realized eschatology, becomes in the additions of John 2 literal and carnal, dependent upon ritual and a future judgment. We know that this is the case, that the Eucharistic passage in John 6:51-58 was added, because it makes meaningless Jesus' response to those who were outraged at his claim of heavenly origin: "What if you see the Son of Man ascending to the place where he was before?" (John 6:62) This is a perfectly adequate response to "How can he now say, 'I have come down from heaven'?" It is no response at all to "'Whoever eats my flesh and drinks my blood" (John 6:56). A great mind's spiritual vision has been muddied by a lesser mind's concern with ritual and future eschatology. This brings us to a consideration of the mind of John 2.

IX

The Mind of John 2

THE SECOND MOST REVEALING AUTHORIAL statement in the gospels, after Luke's preface to Theophilus, is the following passage:

> Peter looked round, and saw the disciple whom Jesus loved following—the one who at supper had leaned back close to him to ask the question, "Lord, who is it that will betray you?" When he caught sight of him, Peter asked, "Lord, what will happen to him?" Jesus said, "If it should be my will that he wait until I come, what is it to you? Follow me."
>
> That saying of Jesus became current in the brotherhood, and was taken to mean that that disciple would not die. But in fact Jesus did not say that he would not die; he only said, "If it should be my will that he wait until I come, what is it to you?" It is this same disciple who attests what has here been written. It is in fact he who wrote it, and we know that his testimony is true. (John 21:20-24)

The writer of the twenty-first chapter of John tells us that he is not the author of the rest of the Fourth Gospel, that someone else, the Beloved Disciple, wrote it. The author of this final, added chapter of John carefully distinguishes himself from that figure, calling himself "we" (as he also does in his own preface at 1:14). It is not hard to conclude that he speaks for a Christian community that possesses an anonymous copy of a gospel it reveres and attributes to an intimate personal associate of Jesus, one whom Jesus loved and even adopted into his own family, instructing his mother, "there is your son," and that disciple, "there is your mother" (John 19:27). Yet very strangely, even though the author of the twenty-first chapter of John seems to know so much about this disciple whom Jesus loved, that disciple is never given a name, and he remains anonymous to this day. How can this be?

We can move toward an answer using the Gospel of Luke, whose preface gives us the other most revealing authorial statement in gospel literature. As her opening words to Theophilus show, Luke believed that her sources—the main one being the gospel we now call Mark—came down to her from the time of personal associates of Jesus—"original eye-witnesses and servants of the Gospel," as she calls them (Luke 1:2). We now know that in this view Luke was wrong, that Mark as she had it was the end product of some forty years of oral traditions about Jesus, and that, rather than being an eyewitness of Jesus, its author was in fact ignorant even of the outline of Jesus' career, beyond the obvious surmise that his baptism came at the beginning and crucifixion at the end. Nonetheless, Luke believed that her sources came from eyewitnesses and that this fact thus guaranteed their reliability. But now comes the paradoxical part: even though her sources had the stamp of "eyewitnesses," they still were not good enough, had somehow got the story of Jesus wrong and needed to be replaced or superseded. Luke has got to do it again—even though "many writers" had already "undertaken to draw up an account" of Jesus' career—"so as to give you authentic knowledge" about Jesus (Luke 1:1-4). Luke is simultaneously protective of and tendentious toward her sources; her confidence in their reliability is joined with an equal confidence in her own ability to revise them so as to be "authentic." This complex attitude probably relates to the anonymity of her sources, their coming from a past that is revered but unknown. For though Luke tells stories in the Book of Acts about John Mark—the personal associate of Peter and Paul—it never occurs to her to relate this figure to the gospel she uses as her main source in her first volume; the Gospel of Mark was as anonymous to her as it is to us. We can now see the relevance of this to the author of the twenty-first chapter of John, whose Christian community also possessed a gospel that it revered as coming out of the past and that was thought to be written by an eyewitness of Jesus, a gospel that was as anonymous to them as Mark was to Luke. The author of the twenty-first chapter of John does not give a name to the person he thought wrote that gospel, *because he doesn't know his name.* The author of this final chapter of John (I shall call him John 2, though others, such as Rudolf Bultmann, have called him "the Redactor") possessed an anonymous gospel which he revised and expanded, adding that last chapter and other material, believing that though this gospel came (as Luke believed of the Gospel of Mark) from an eyewitness of Jesus, it nonetheless presented a theological understanding of Jesus that needed correction: it downplayed the sacraments, especially baptism and the Eucharist, it presented an almost docetic view of Jesus (that his flesh was only apparent, not real), and worst of all, it tried mightily to destroy the revered Christian tradition of future eschatology—of a Jesus coming again to judge. The work we now call the Gospel of John is a revised and expanded edition of a lost gospel, of an anonymous book that no longer exists as first written by that nameless figure whom John 2 mistakenly identified as an eyewitness of Jesus. Just as Luke assumed that Mark would become a lost gospel after she had revised and absorbed it into her own work (and it almost did, as there exists no second-century copy of Mark and only one third-century copy), so did John 2 assume the same, and correctly: we do not possess the work that absorbed the Signs Gospel and became the anonymous gospel that John 2 revised. We cannot know what John 2 removed, but we can certainly look at what he has *added*, since chapter 21 is a frank implicit admission that additions have been made. The rest of this chapter is about those additions and revisions.

We can best start by looking again at that passage in the twenty-first chapter about the Beloved Disciple. There is something strange in the author's quibble about a saying of Jesus that he acknowledges was widespread but insists was misunderstood. There were Christians, he says, who thought, on the basis of a saying that was "current in the brotherhood," that the Beloved Disciple "would not die." That the saying had become problematic to John 2 clearly means that this nameless person, indeed his whole generation, has indeed died, is so dead and gone that John 2 does not even know his name. And such sayings certainly were common in the first century; Mark's Christian community preserved one very similar, in which Jesus assured his followers that "there are some of those standing here who will not taste death before they have seen the kingdom of God already come in power" (Mark 9:1). Mark wrote this soon after 70 C.E., believing that the seventies were the outer limit of the lives of Jesus' contemporaries and that the parousia and the kingdom were imminent. By Mark's lights, the saying made perfect sense; but a generation or so later, when John 2 was writing, such sayings made no sense at all and needed major revision. Admittedly the revision John 2 attempted is an unconvincing quibble, but it is basic to his purpose: he writes that Jesus did not in fact say that one of his intimate circle would live until the Second Coming, but rather that Jesus *could* keep him alive until the Second Coming if he wanted to do so (though since he and his whole generation were dead Jesus obviously had not wanted to do so). John 2 is facing the same problem the author of II Peter faced—a threat to faith in the Second Coming stemming from its failure to happen: "Note this first: in the last days there will come men who scoff at religion and live self indulgent lives, and they will say: 'Where now is the promise of his coming? Our fathers have been laid to their rest, but still everything continues exactly as it has always been since the world began'" (II Peter 3:3-4). The revisionist strategy of John 2 may at least be more convincing than the one attempted here by the author of II Peter, for whom unbelief in the imminence of the parousia was somehow proof that the parousia was imminent.

Indeed the failure of Jesus to return within the lifetimes of his first followers was a problem for John 2; in his view the belief that Jesus had said "that that disciple would not die" *must* have been a misunderstanding, for the prediction and its failure could call into question the whole idea of the Second Coming, as it clearly did for those "scoffers" attacked in II Peter. Moreover, John 2 was himself a strong believer in future eschatology, part of a Christian community convinced that "this is the last hour" (I John 2:18), and was trying to save the belief by re-interpreting the saying. But unfortunately this (supposedly misunderstood) saying, that the Beloved Disciple "would not die," was not the only thing needing re-interpretation: *all* of the anonymous gospel supposedly written by that now-dead Beloved Disciple centers on this very same idea: "no one who is alive and has faith shall ever die" (John 11:26); "if anyone obeys my teaching he shall never know what it is to die" (John 8:51). John 2 has a much bigger problem than one isolated "misunderstood" saying; and indeed his re-interpretation of that saying is part of his strategy for revision of the entire anonymous gospel he both revered and needed to change. He had to put future eschatology back into a gospel that had tried to destroy it, and his revisions were substantial.

Fortunately for us those revisions are often easy to spot, being awkward and illogical, running against the grain of John's original intent. Start, for example, with the story of Lazarus. John's point had been that Martha's hope for a "resurrection on the last day" (11:24) was superfluous; no one need wait that long, for Jesus himself *is* the resurrection, Jesus *is* life (11:25); "no one who is alive and has faith will ever die" (11:26). This is a central theme in the work of John, sounding very much like that supposedly misunderstood saying in chapter 21, and John 2 found it as problematic as "that disciple would not die." For him, as for Martha, eternal life is something that comes *after* "resurrection on the last day," not just some metaphorical spiritual quality in the present life of the believer; so he has to play down John's original point, that "resurrection" is a metaphor for the life of the believer who has "already passed from death to life" (John 5:24), and rescue Martha's more traditional belief. His success is only marginal, for we find ourselves taken aback to find that in the same breath with which Jesus tells Martha that "no one...who has faith shall ever die," he also says "If a man has faith in me, even though he die, he shall come to life" (John 11:25). If one will not "ever die," how can one "die"? The revision attempted by John 2 of John's realized eschatology reduces Jesus' great speech to nonsense. This effort to re-insert a "last day" theology into a context that had tried to destroy it is never quite successful, as John 2 seems afraid to tamper too much with his Beloved Disciple's work. Earlier, back in the fifth chapter, John 2 reveals the same ineptness. John had written that Jesus declared that anyone who "puts his faith in him who sent me has hold of eternal life, and does not come up for judgment, but has already passed from death to life. In truth, in very truth I tell you, a time is coming, indeed it is already here, when the dead shall hear the voice of the Son of God, and all who hear shall come to life" (John 5:24-25).

We are again taken aback when we continue reading, to find that in the very next breath after saying that resurrection and eternal life for believers is *now*, since believers do "not come up for judgment," John 2's Jesus goes on to say, "As Son of Man, he has also been given the right to pass judgment. Do not wonder at this, because the time is coming when all who are in the grave shall hear his voice and come out: those who have done right will rise to life; those who have done wrong will rise to their doom" (John 5:27-29).

A denial of future eschatology is followed by an assertion of future eschatology. The conflict of "no judgment/future judgment" runs throughout the revisions made by John 2. John the universalist had made Jesus declare that "I have not come to judge the world but to save the world" (12:47); John 2 comes along behind to make Jesus assert that "the word that I spoke will be his judge on the last day" (12:49). John had made Jesus declare that "the Son can do nothing by himself; he does only what he sees the Father doing" (5:19); John 2 comes along behind him to insert "the Father does not judge anyone, but has given full jurisdiction to the Son" (5:22).

Not only does John 2 clumsily re-introduce future eschatology into the anonymous gospel he possessed, he does the same with the sacraments of baptism and the Eucharist. John had as little interest in rituals as he did in "signs," seeing both as externalities, "carnal'" things that got in the way of the spiritual. Indeed, John had so little interest in the ritual of baptism that he neglected entirely to mention that Jesus had been immersed by John the Baptist; instead he reduces that figure's role to merely pointing at Jesus, who will replace him and his function. The "Lamb of God, who takes away the sins of the world," will render superfluous John's ritual ("to baptize in water"), replacing it with a new, non-ritual activity: "to baptize in the Holy Spirit" (John 1:29,33). On the other hand, the ritual of baptism was highly significant to John 2, as we can see in his revision of Jesus' encounter with Nicodemus. For John, to "see the kingdom of God" requires that one be "born from above," or "born again," as Jesus tells Nicodemus (*gennēthē anōthen* is deliberately ambiguous, and can mean either). Nicodemus, who is impressed by Jesus for the wrong reason— "these signs of yours"— interprets Jesus' words carnally, in terms of physical birth ("Can he enter his mother's womb a second time?"—3:4), whereas Jesus had intended the spiritual meaning: "Flesh can give birth only to flesh; it is spirit that gives birth to spirit" (3:6). So for John, "rebirth" is a purely spiritual matter, nothing physical is involved; but John 2 clumsily re-introduces a physical matter into the scene—the ritual of baptism—by inserting two words, "water and," into Jesus' first answer to Nicodemus' carnal misunderstanding of "born from above": "In truth I tell you, no one can enter the kingdom of God without being born from water and spirit" (3:5). But "water" contradicts the point of the rest of the speech, being unambiguous and physical, whereas the speech itself deliberately exploits the ambiguities of *anōthen* ("from above," or "again") and *pneuma* ("spirit," or "wind"):

> Flesh can give birth only to flesh; it is spirit [not "water and spirit"] that gives birth to spirit. You ought not to be astonished, then, when I tell you that you must be born over again. The wind [or spirit] blows where it wills; you hear the sound of it, but you do not know where it comes from, or where it is going. So with everyone who is born from spirit." (John 3:6-8)

Again, there is no mention of "water and" in this last sentence; John 2 added it in verse 5 but neglected to add it in verse 8, so that the pair of words jars against its context, one that clearly renders ritual and the physical superfluous.

John possessed a mind that was extraordinarily subtle, one that reveled in metaphor and ambiguity and loved to contrast Jesus with literal-minded people who misunderstood his profound statements. John 2, on the other hand, had a much more pedestrian mind, and sometimes fell into the same kind of literal-minded muddle that caught Nicodemus. John had exploited the double meaning of "baptize," contrasting the old literal ritual of John the Baptist with Jesus' new, more subtle baptizing in Holy Spirit. But John 2 then tried to turn Jesus back into another John the Baptist: "Jesus went into Judea with his disciples, stayed there with them, and baptized" (John 3:22); but John's point (which John 2 failed to excise) was that "it was only the disciples who were baptizing, and not Jesus himself" (John 4:2). John used water as a symbol, not for baptism, but for Jesus' words of life, as in the episode of the Samaritan woman at the well. Here again John enjoys contrasting Jesus' subtle wordplay against an ordinary person's literal-mindedness. When Jesus tells the Samaritan woman that he could give her "living water," she fails to grasp that he speaks metaphorically: "Sir, you have no bucket and this well is deep" (4:10-11). Of course Jesus did not mean literal water, even of baptism: "The water that I shall give will be an inner spring always welling up for eternal life" (4:14). But the woman remains stubbornly literal-minded, demanding "that water, and then I shall not be thirsty, nor have to come all this way to draw" (4:15).

Perhaps the best example of a scene that, when analyzed, shows the difference between John and his reviser is the great "bread of life" speech in chapter 6. John characteristically employed a miracle story out of the Signs Gospel as merely the occasion for a great discourse of Jesus in which he stresses that "signs," in themselves, are of little import, being only pointers to, symbols of, the reality, Jesus himself. Human nature, on the other hand, is only too ready to value the symbol more than the reality; so Jesus tells his audience "You must work, not for this perishable food, but for the food that lasts, the food of eternal life. This food the Son of Man will give you" (John 6:27). As usual, John's Jesus is speaking metaphorically; the *real* "bread from heaven" is neither the manna of Moses nor the loaves and fishes of the Signs Gospel. Rather, "The bread that God gives comes down from heaven and brings life to the world" (John 6:33). Like the Samaritan woman, this audience too still thinks of literal food: "Sir, give us this bread," but Jesus confounds them with a profound symbolism: "I am the bread of life. Whoever comes to me shall never be hungry, and whoever believes in me shall never be thirsty. But you, as I said, do not believe although you have seen" (6:33-36). Jesus' hearers not only misunderstand his metaphor, they take offense at his claim of origin: "I have come down from heaven, not to do my own will, but the will of him who sent me...For it is my Father's will that everyone who looks upon the Son and puts his faith in him shall possess eternal life" (6:38,40). Not the carnal act of eating but the spiritual act of believing in Jesus is the source of life, says John's Jesus. And once again his hearers miss the point:

> At this the Jews began to murmur disapprovingly because he said, "I am the bread which came down from heaven." They said, "Surely this is Jesus son of Joseph; we know his father and mother. How can he now say, 'I have come down from heaven'?" (6:41-42)

Then along comes John 2 a few years later and once again, like Jesus' audience in John, turns life back into a matter of eating and drinking, reversing spiritual metaphors back into carnal acts. As the metaphorical living water of John became the literal water of baptism of John 2, so the metaphorical bread of life of John becomes the elements of the Eucharist of John 2, as he adds a shockingly carnal passage to the great discourse in his source:

> I am that living bread which has come down from heaven; if anyone eats this bread he shall live for ever. Moreover, the bread which I will give is my own flesh; I give it for the life of the world...Whoever eats my flesh and drinks my blood possesses eternal life, and I will raise him up on the last day. My flesh is real food; my blood is real drink. Whoever eats my flesh and drinks my blood dwells continually in me and I dwell in him. (John 6:51,54-56)

John 2 re-inserts last-day eschatology, eucharistic literalism, and a gruesomely physical interpretation of the indwelling of deity into a passage that had pointed in just the opposite direction. We can know that this whole passage about "he who eats me shall live" was added by a later hand, because Jesus' response to the outrage his speech has evoked is the response John had given to "I have come down from heaven," and is in no way a response to "he who eats me": "Does this shock you? What if you see the Son of Man ascending to the place where he was before? The spirit alone gives life; the flesh is of no avail; the words I have spoken to you are both spirit and life" (John 6:62-63). If "the flesh is of no avail," then how can the "bread" Jesus gives be "my own flesh"? John's point was that Jesus' *words* were the metaphoric bread, and faith in those words was metaphoric "eating" of his message, while the point John 2 wishes to make concerns a ritual of the church and a belief in a last-day eschatology. While John had argued that mere "faith in the Son" brings eternal life, John 2 argued that participation in a ritual of eating and drinking brings eternal life "on the last day." But John 2 failed to notice that Jesus' response in 6:62-63 was not a response to "he who eats me" and in fact belies the whole point of the insertion; the flesh is indeed of no avail, faith in Jesus, not eating and drinking, is John's point so woefully missed by the literal-minded John 2.

Now, if it is indeed true, as John argued, that "the spirit alone gives life; the flesh is of no avail," what are we to make of the great passage in the preface to the Fourth Gospel, "the Word became flesh"? Here is the key to what lay behind the need John 2 felt to revise his great source so radically. There were Christians known to John 2 for whom Jesus' flesh was a genuine scandal, the very same kind of Christians John 2 places in his addition to the "bread of life" speech: "Many of his disciples on hearing it exclaimed, "This is more than we can stomach! Why listen to such talk?"…From that time on, many of his disciples withdrew and no longer went about with him" (John 6:60, 66). John 2 in fact knew about and was opposed to this very same kind of Christian—those appalled at the very idea of Jesus' flesh and eating it. For indeed there had been a split in his own Christian community over this same issue—we know about it from the letters of John in the New Testament—and his revision of the anonymous gospel he possessed is part of his effort to deal with that split. Realizing that this anonymous gospel—one he really thought had been written by an eyewitness of Jesus—with its nearly docetic view of Jesus and its consistent downgrading of flesh, could in fact be used, was being used, by those very Christians (Valentinus and Heracleon did that very thing), John 2 set about revising it, salting it with key references to the Incarnation, to Jesus' flesh and to eating that flesh. A gospel that had tried to argue that "flesh is of no avail" (John 6:63) was re-written to insist that the "Word became flesh" and that only the one who eats his flesh will possess eternal life. The anonymous gospel that John 2 thought had been written by an eyewitness of Jesus had set itself upon a trajectory that had culminated in docetism and gnosticism, departing from mainstream

Christianity. John 2 hit upon the brilliant ploy of using that very gospel to bring readers of it back into the mainstream; in doing so he asserts not only the centrality of the Incarnation, he also works to restore Peter—and thus mainstream, Petrine Christianity—to the center of his newly-revised gospel.

The sentence that tells of those disciples who "withdrew" from Jesus over the question of his flesh is followed by John 2's first effort to re-instate Peter at the center of Christianity: "So Jesus asked the Twelve, 'Do you also want to leave me?' Simon Peter answered him, 'Lord, to whom shall we go? Your words are words of eternal life. We have faith, and we know that you are the Holy One of God'" (John 6:67-69). The Beloved Disciple momentarily vanishes, replaced by Peter, who has now become the spokesman for those who "have faith" in Jesus' flesh and in the value of eating it; the ones who "withdrew" are the ones lacking such faith. John 2 struggles mightily to recast an anonymous gospel that declared that "flesh is of no avail" (John 6:63) into one that honors both Peter and the ritual of the Eucharist. That effort to re-instate Peter culminates in the twenty-first chapter, where he is fully restored as leader of the church.

Like most of the rest of John 2's revisions, this last chapter forms an extremely awkward addition. The final chapter of John's work had presented Jesus' commission to his disciples: "'As the Father sent me, so I send you'. Then he breathed on them, saying, 'Receive the Holy Spirit!'" (John 20:21-22). But when he added the final chapter, John 2 showed them acting as if they had never received any such commission and have returned to their old profession of fishing: "So they started and got into the boat. But that night they caught nothing. Morning came, and there stood Jesus on the beach, but the disciples did not know that it was Jesus" (John 21:3-4). But in the previous chapter—John's concluding one—the disciples recognize the resurrected Jesus immediately, and are "filled with joy" (John 20:20). John 2 has forgotten this, possibly under the influence of Luke's scene on the road to Emmaus, where "something kept" the two disciples "from seeing who it was" when the risen Jesus appeared (Luke 24:16).

John 2 continues by describing those present: "Simon Peter [named first!] and Thomas 'the Twin' were together with Nathanael of Cana-in-Galilee. The sons of Zebedee and two other disciples were also there" (John 21:2). John 2 has forgotten that "the sons of Zebedee" is a Synoptic term; James and John are never called by this term elsewhere in the Fourth Gospel. The Redactor's hand is already clearly apparent in the first two verses of his added chapter. The two "other disciples" must remain anonymous because John 2 does not know the name of the figure John had consistently left nameless—the Beloved Disciple—so in this account at least one participant must stand for that figure and be given no name.

As they fish unsuccessfully, the still unrecognized Jesus tells them to "Shoot the net to starboard." "They did so, and found they could not haul the net aboard, there were so many fish in it. Then the disciple whom Jesus loved said to Peter, 'It is the Lord!'" (John 21:5-7). John 2 has borrowed a scene from Luke, or from the same oral tradition that Luke used, to begin his restoration of Peter as head of the church. Luke places her version of this scene early in Jesus' career, not after the resurrection, as does John 2:

> When he had finished speaking, he said to Simon, "Put out into deep water and let down your nets for a catch." Simon answered, "Master, we were hard at work all night and caught nothing at all; but if you say so, I will let down the nets." They did so and made a great haul of fish; and their nets began to split....When Simon saw what had happened he fell at Jesus' knees and said, "Go, Lord, leave me, sinner that I am!" For he and all his companions were amazed at the catch they had made; so too were his partners James and John, Zebedee's sons. "Do not be afraid," said Jesus to Simon, "from now on you will be catching men." (Luke 5:4-10)

Luke's scene grants primacy to Peter, the fisher of men, whose own sense of unworthiness is overcome by Jesus' commission to him. John 2 uses the scene to the same end: "When Peter heard that ['It is the Lord!'], he wrapped his coat about him (for he had stripped) and plunged into the sea. The rest of them came on in the boat, towing the net full of fish" (John 21:7-8).

Peter becomes once again, in the chapter added by John 2, the impetuous figure of the Synoptics rather than the laggard of John's lost Gospel.

Peter, the first to respond with wild joy at seeing Jesus again, becomes the center of the next scene, where love between Jesus and Peter, rather than between Jesus and the Beloved Disciple, becomes the distinguishing characteristic of the newly-reinstated Rock: "Simon son of John, do you love me more than all else?" a question thrice asked and thrice answered positively, each time as the basis for the command, "Feed/tend my sheep" (John 21:15-17). Not the Beloved Disciple, but Peter, will be the shepherd of Jesus' flock. Moreover, it is Peter who will have the honor to be martyred for Jesus, not the Beloved Disciple, who will live on rather than glorifying God with his death: "'when you are old you will stretch out your arms, and a stranger will bind you fast, and carry you where you have no wish to go.' He said this to indicate the manner of death by which Peter was to glorify God. Then he added, 'Follow me'" (John 21:18-19). And whereas Peter at the Last Supper had to go through the Beloved Disciple in order to learn the identity of the betrayer, this time Peter directly asks Jesus about the fate of the Beloved Disciple; Peter becomes once again our mediator to Jesus:

> Peter looked round and saw the disciple whom Jesus loved following—the one who at supper had leaned back close to him to ask the question, "Lord, who is it that will betray you?" When he caught sight of him, Peter asked, "Lord, what will happen to him?" Jesus said, "If it should be my will that he wait until I come, what is that to you? Follow me." (John 21:20-22)

Thus the readers of this added chapter are expected to accept Peter's superior role of glorifying God by his martyrdom and the Beloved Disciple's lesser role of living on as one of those who heard Jesus' command to Peter that he feed his sheep. This last chapter is intended to show that nothing the Beloved Disciple was thought to have written could overshadow Peter's primacy among the apostles. With that, John 2 proceeds to undercut the "misunderstanding" of those who thought that "that disciple would not die," a revision that helped save future eschatology and ultimately allowed the Fourth Gospel to be accepted by mainstream Christianity.

Can we discover the context of this revision, its time and place? The rest of this chapter will make that effort, arguing that though the Fourth Gospel was first written in Alexandria, it was re-written in Ephesus; the Alexandrian version has become a lost gospel, we have only the Ephesian. Since late in the second century, Ephesus has been accepted in Christian tradition as the city where this gospel was written by John the son of Zebedee, and though modern critical scholarship no longer takes serious-ly the idea that the Fourth Gospel comes from this eyewitness, we still need to look closely at the identification of Ephesus as its place of origin. Not long before the year 200, Irenaeus, Bishop of Lyon, wrote in his book *Against the Heretics* that "John, the disciple of the Lord, who also had leaned upon his breast, did himself publish a Gospel during his residence at Ephesus in Asia" (*Adv. Haer.* 3.1.1). At the very least this must mean there was an early association between the Fourth Gospel and the city of Ephesus. But we need to note that part of the purpose of Irenaeus was to attack the teachings of Cerinthus, a gnostic Christian teacher who lived in Ephesus at the end of the first century. This Cerinthus, who "was educat-ed in the wisdom of the Egyptians, taught that the world was not made by the primary God, but by a certain Power far separated from him…Moreover, after [Jesus'] baptism, Christ descended upon him in the form of a dove from the Supreme Ruler, and that then he proclaimed the unknown Father, and performed miracles. But at last Christ departed from Jesus, and that then Jesus suffered and rose again, while Christ remained impassable, inasmuch as he was a spiritual being" (1.26.1). Irenaeus went on to declare that John at Ephesus sought,

> by the proclamation of the Gospel, to remove that error which by Cerinthus had been disseminated among men, and a long time previously by those termed Nicolaitans, who are an offset of that "knowledge" [*gnosis*] falsely so called, that he might confound them, and persuade them that there is but one God, who made all things by His Word; and not, as they allege, that the Creator was one, but the Father of the Lord another; and that the Son of the Creator was, forsooth, one, but the Christ from above another. (3.11.1)

So the gospel attributed, late in the second century, to John at Ephesus was viewed as an anti-gnostic, anti-Cerinthean work. But, very strangely, Epiphanius, in *his* book against the heretics, argues against those who actually believed that it was Cerinthus himself who wrote the Gospel of John! (*Adv. Haeres.* 51.3.6). How could it be that the Fourth Gospel was at one time in its history regarded as the product of an Egyptian-trained gnostic, and at another time in its history regarded as composed for the very purpose of attacking this same gnostic? I think the answer is plausible that in an early, now-lost version, the Fourth Gospel could well have been read in a Cerinthean, gnostic fashion, but that at Ephesus a revision of it was produced (we now call it the Gospel of John) that put this gospel back into the Christian mainstream. Is there evidence of an early Christian group that seemed to have two conflicting interpretations (or even versions) of the Fourth Gospel? I think there is, and we can find it in the letters of John, works generally accepted as having been written right at the end of the first century to churches in and around Ephesus. We need not accept Willi Marxsen's notion that the author of the First Letter of John was the same person as John 2, whom he calls "the Redactor" (1968, 262), but it is widely held that the three letters attributed to John stem from Christian communities that revered and used the Fourth Gospel (Brown, 1979, 106). But sometime around the end of the first century those communities were afflicted with turmoil and schism: "My children, this is the last hour! You were told that Antichrist was to come, and now many antichrists have appeared; which proves to us that this is indeed the last hour. They went out from our company, but never really belonged to us" (I John 2:18-19). The author or authors of the Johannine letters have a precise meaning for "Antichrist," a word that occurs only in the First and Second letters of John: "Many deceivers have gone out into the world, who do not acknowledge Jesus Christ as coming in the flesh. These are the persons described as the Antichrist" (2 John 7).

Some members of the Johannine community departed, became a rival sect, over the question of the "flesh" of Jesus Christ, an event that leads the author of I John to certainty that "this is the last hour." We do not know for sure who these secessionists were, but as Raymond Brown notes, they were "not detectably outsiders to the Johannine community but the offspring of Johannine thought itself, justifying their positions by the

Johannine Gospel and its implications" (1979, 107). This seems likely, until we reflect on the oddity of people who purportedly deny that "Jesus Christ came in the flesh" citing a gospel that declares "the Word became flesh," and "whoever eats my flesh and drinks my blood possesses eternal life." Brown's arguments founder on his insistence that "John *exactly as we have it*" (108, his italics) was the text used by those who left the Johannine community. Brown refuses to "exclude certain passages from the Fourth Gospel on the grounds that they were probably not in the tradition known to the secessionists but were added by the redactor (either later or as anti-secessionist revision)" (1979, 109). He admits that many accept that John 1:14—"The Word became flesh"—was "added by the redactor as an attack on the opponents of I John" (1979, 109) but continues to write as if there were no revision of the Fourth Gospel.

Brown has it exactly backwards. Irenaeus had a real point in suggesting that someone in Ephesus around 100 C.E. wrote in order to refute Cerinthus and the Nicolaitans, and that what he produced we now call the Fourth Gospel. Irenaeus only missed that this author was revising an earlier, anonymous gospel, the work of John. The Ephesian author (I call him John 2) was dealing with the same kind of unorthodox Christians who left the Johannine churches, and who used (I argue) an earlier, now-lost version of the Fourth Gospel. John 2 even described them; they were the kind of people who wondered "How can this man give us his flesh to eat?", people who were appalled at the very idea of Jesus Christ's flesh and eating it: "This is more than we can stomach," they said, and "withdrew, and no longer went about with him" (John 6:52, 60, 66).

John 2 is describing a division in his own Christian community; those who "withdrew" represent the very kind of Christian he was writing against, followers of Cerinthus and the Nicolaitans, as Irenaeus said. This last-named group gives us the key to the place where all this was happening; for the Nicolaitans were prominent, in the nineties of the first century, in Asia Minor, in the cities of Ephesus and Pergamum, as we know from the opening letters to the churches in the Book of Revelation:

IX: The Mind of John 2

To the angel of the church at Ephesus write:...I know you cannot endure evil men; you have put to the proof those who claim to be apostles, but are not, and have found them to be false....Yet you have this in your favor: you hate the practices of the Nicolaitans, as I do. (Rev. 2:1,2,6) To the angel of the church at Pergamum write:....you also have some who hold the doctrine of the Nicolaitans. So repent! (Rev. 2:12,15)

It is generally held that Revelation was written in the mid-nineties of the first century, by which time Ephesus had, it would seem, rid itself of Nicolaitans, though Pergamum (a hundred miles to the north) had not. The three letters of John, traditionally connected to Ephesus in Asia Minor, are written also to churches only partially free of an unorthodox group, that appeared to be claiming the apostolic authority of (something like) the Johannine Gospel. If the situations are one and the same, my case rests.

"Evanished All and Gone"?

*M*ATTHEW *and Mark and Luke and holy John*
Evanished all and gone!
Yea, he that erst, his dusky curtains quitting,
Through Eastern pictured panes his level beams transmitting,
With gorgeous portraits blent,
On them his glories intercepted spent,
Southwestering now, through windows plainly glassed,
On the inside face his radiance keenly cast,
And in the luster lost, invisible and gone,
Are, say you, Matthew, Mark and Luke and holy John?
Lost, is it? lost, to be recovered never?
However, The place of worship the meantime with light
Is, if less richly, more sincerely bright,
And in blue skies the Orb is manifest to sight.

—Arthur Hugh Clough, "Epi-strauss-ium," 1847

The clotted syntax and rough, unpretty rhythms of Arthur Hugh Clough's poem, "Epi-strauss-ium" ("Concerning Strauss-ism"), give a vivid impression of the distress and sense of loss nineteenth-century readers felt when they grasped the implications of David Friederich Strauss's pioneering work of biblical criticism, *Das Leben Jesu*. George Eliot had translated the work into English in 1847 as *The Life of Jesus*. Clough read it and responded with the anguished but hopeful poem quoted above. Now, a century and a half later, Clough's muted optimism about the benefits of biblical scholarship has still not trickled down to general English or American readers, who know little about its findings.

Clough had hoped that Strauss's work, which had identified major parts of the gospels' stories as "myths," would make the place of worship, the church itself, "more sincerely bright," with less room for dark illusions. Though the "gorgeous portraits" of the four Evangelists—traditionally pictured in church windows as ox, eagle, lion, and man—had in a sense vanished in the clear light of biblical criticism, the result, he hoped, was an unobstructed view of the sun itself from each pew.

Clough saw himself standing in the afternoon of Christian history, observing the "Orb" of the sun through "plainly glassed" western windows clearly for the first time, the truth about the past finally revealed by such scholars as Strauss. Clough had grasped the genuine paradox inherent in the findings of modern biblical scholarship: that though it may seem to make "Matthew and Mark and Luke and holy John" disappear, it actually renders them more transparent, more full of light. The windows continue to need regular cleaning.

Bibliography

Anchor Bible Dictionary, ed. David Noel Freedman. New York: Doubleday, 1992.

The Ante-Nicene Fathers, 10 vols. ed. Alexander Roberts. Grand Rapids: Eerdmans, 1973 (for Epiphanius and Irenaeus).

Barrett, C. K. *The Gospel According to St. John*. Philadelphia: Westminster, 1978.

Berry, George Ricker. *The Classic Greek Dictionary*. Chicago: Follett, 1958.

Bevan, Edwyn R. *The House of Seleucus: A History of the Hellenistic Near East Under the Seleucid Dynasty*. Chicago: Ares, 1985 (rept. of 1902 ed.).

Bovon, Francois. "The Synoptic Gospels and the Noncanonical Acts of the Apostles," *Harvard Theological Review* 81, 1988, 19-36.

Brown, Raymond E. *The Birth of the Messiah*. New York: Doubleday, 1977.

———. *The Community of the Beloved Disciple*. New York: Paulist Press, 1979.

———. *The Gospel According to John*. 2 vols. New York: Doubleday, 1970.

Budge, E. A. Wallis. *The Book the Dead: The Papyrus of Ani*. New York: Dover, 1967.

———. *The Book of the Opening of the Mouth*. New York: Blom, 1972.

Bultmann, Rudolf. *Existence and Faith: Shorter Writings of Rudolf Bultmann*. Schubert M. Ogden (Trans). Cleveland: Meridian, 1960.

———. *The History of the Synoptic Tradition*. trans. John Marsh. New York: Harper, 1976.

———. *The Gospel of John*. Philadelphia: Westminster, 1971.

Conzelmann, Hans, and Andreas Lindemann. *Interpreting the New Testament*. Peabody, Mass.: Hendrickson, 1988.

Crossan, John Dominic. *The Historical Jesus: The Life of a Mediterranean Jewish Peasant*. San Francisco: Harper, 1991.

———. *Who Killed Jesus?* San Francisco: Harper, 1995.

Curry, Neil, trans. *Euripides*. Cambridge: Cambridge Univ. Press, 1981.

Dodd, C.H. *The Parables of the Kingdom*. New York: Scribner, 1961 (1936).

Dodds, E. R. *Euripides: Bacchae*. Oxford: Clarendon, 1960.

Eusebius, Pamphili. *History of the Church*, trans. G. A. Williamson. Harmondsworth, England: Penguin, 1960.

Faulkner, R. O. *The Ancient Egyptian Pyramid Texts*. Oxford: Clarendon, 1969.

Flender, H. *St. Luke: Theologian of Redemptive History*. London: SPCK, 1967.

Fortna, Robert. *The Fourth Gospel and its Predecessor*. New York: Columbia, 1988.

Frye, Northrop. *The Great Code: The Bible and Literature*. New York: Harcourt Brace, 1982.

Funk, Robert W. "On Distinguishing Historical Fiction From Fictive Narrative," *Forum: A Journal of the Foundations & Facets of Western Culture*. 9, no. 3., 1997, 179-216.

Funk, Robert W. and Roy W. Hoover, eds. *The Five Gospels: The Search For the Authentic Words* of *Jesus*. New York: Polebridge Press, 1993.

Grene, David, and Richmond Lattimore. *The Complete Greek Tragedies, Vol. IV: Euripides*. Chicago: Univ. of Chicago Press, 1960.

Gundry, Robert Horton. *Matthew: A Commentary on His Literary and Theological Art*. Grand Rapids: Eerdmans, 1982.

Haenchen, Ernst. *The Acts of the Apostles: A Commentary*. Philadelphia: Westminster, 1971.

———. *John: A Commentary*, Robert W. Funk (Trans). Philadelphia: Fortress, 1984. 2 vols.

Hanson, Paul D. *Old Testament Apocalyptic*. Philadelphia: Westminster, 1987.

Helms, Randel. *Gospel Fictions*. Buffalo: Prometheus, 1988.

Interpreter's Dictionary of the Bible, 4 vols. ed. George Arthur Buttrick et al. New York: Abingdon, 1962.

Jacobson, Arland D. "The Sayings Gospel Q," in *The Complete Gospels*, Robert J. Miller (ed.), 1992, 249-300.

Josephus, Flavius. *The Jewish War*, trans. G. A. Williamson. Harmondsworth, England: Penguin, 1959.

Kaesemann, Ernst. *The Testament of Jesus*. G. Krodel (Trans).
Philadelphia: Westminster, 1968.

Kee, Howard Clark. *Community of the New Age: Studies in Mark's Gospel*.
Philadelphia: Westminster, 1977.

Kloppenborg, John S. *The Formation of* Q. Philadelphia: Fortress, 1987.

Koester, Helmut. *Ancient Christian Gospels: Their History and
Development*. Philadelphia: Trinity Press, 1990.

Kraemer, Ross Shepard. *Her Share of the Blessings: Women's Religions
Among Pagans, Jews, and Christians in the Greco-Roman World*. New
York: Oxford Univ. Press, 1992.

Mack, Burton L. *The Lost Gospel: The Book of* Q *and Christian Origins*.
San Francisco: Harper, 1993.

——. *Who Wrote the New Testament? The Making of the Christian* Myth.
San Francisco: Harper, 1995.

Marxsen, Willi. *Introduction to the New Testament*, trans. G. Buswell.
Philadelphia: Fortress, 1968.

Meier, John P. *A Marginal Jew: Rethinking the Historical Jesus*, vol. I. New
York: Doubleday, 1991.

Miller, Robert J., ed. *The Complete Gospels*. Sonoma: Polebridge
Press, 1992.

Nineham, Dennis E. *Saint Mark*. Baltimore: Penguin, 1963.

Pagels, Elaine H. *The Johannine Gospel in Gnostic Exegesis: Heracleon's
Commentary on John*. Nashville: Abingdon, 1973.

——. *The Origin of Satan*. New York: Random House, 1995.

Robinson, James M., ed. *The Nag Hammadi Library in English*. San
Francisco: Harper & Row, 1988.

Schüssler Fiorenza, Elisabeth. *In Memory of Her: A Feminist Theological
Reconstruction of Christian Origins*. New York: Crossroad, 1994 (Tenth
Anniversary Edition).

——. ed. *Searching the Scriptures: A Feminist Commentary*, 2 vols. New
York: Crossroad, 1993.

Seim, Turid Karlsen. "The Gospel of Luke," in Schüssler Fiorenza. *Searching
the Scriptures: A Feminist Commentary*. New York: Crossroad, 1994.

Bibliography

Smith, Morton. *The Secret Gospel of Mark*. New York: Columbia Univ.
  Press, 1973.

Strachan, Robert H. *The Fourth Gospel and its Significance*. London: SCM
  Press, 1941.

Streeter, B. H. *The Four Gospels: A Study of Origins*. London: Macmillan,
  1951.

Tannehill, Robert C. *The Narrative Unity of Luke-Acts*. Philadelphia:
  Fortress, 1986.

Wrede, Wilhelm. *The Messianic Secret*. trans. J.C.G. Greig. London:
  SCM, 1971.

Index

Index